Poetry Ireland REVIEW 116

A WB Yeats Special Issue

Eagarthóir/Editor

VONA GROARKE

Poetry Ireland Ltd / Éigse Éireann Teo gratefully acknowledges the assistance of
The Arts Council / An Chomhairle Ealaíon, The Arts Council of Northern Ireland,
Yeats 2015, the Department of Arts, Heritage and the Gaeltacht /
An Roinn Ealaíon, Oidhreachta agus Gaeltachta,
and the Western Development Commission / Coimisiún Forbartha an Iarthair.

Poetry Ireland invites individuals and commercial organisations to become
Friends of Poetry Ireland. For more details please contact:

Poetry Ireland Friends Scheme, Poetry Ireland, 32 Kildare St,
    Dublin 2, Ireland
or telephone +353 1 6789815; e-mail management@poetryireland.ie

FRIENDS:
Joan and Joe McBreen, Desmond Windle, Neville Keery,
Noel and Anne Monahan, Ruth Webster, Maurice Earls,
Mary Shine Thompson, Seán Coyle, Henry and Deirdre Comerford

Poetry Ireland Review is published three times a year by Poetry Ireland Ltd. The Editor
enjoys complete autonomy in the choice of material published. The contents of this
publication should not be taken to reflect either the views or the policy of the publishers.

ISBN: 1-902121-55-4   ISSN: 0332-2998

Prepared for publication by Paul Lenehan and Elizabeth Mohen of Poetry Ireland,
with the assistance of Isabelle Cartwright and Orla Higgins.

DESIGN: Alastair Keady (**www.hexhibit.com**).

COVER CREDIT: *The song remains the same* (collage), by **James Hanley RHA**.

Contents

Poetry Ireland Review 116

Editorial

'Incorrigibly plural', writes Louis MacNeice in 'Snow'. He wasn't writing about Yeats, (I think), but Yeats is so incorrigibly plural that if he'd not had an 's' at the end of his name, we might have to add it anyway.

Pick a Yeats, any Yeats, from his dramatis personae: *Fin de siècle*, Victorian dandy. Republican firebrand. Thwarted lover. Myth-maker. Figurehead. Senator. Enthusiast. Campaigner. Busy-body. Visionary. Delusionary. Fantasist. Family man.

Not to mention, dramatist and essayist. Not to mention, poet. Not to mention, National Poet.

We grow up with Yeats. From the pretty soundtrack of his youth, all harmony and sweet enthusiasms, to the more involved reflections of his middle years, to the barely restrained rage of his extraordinary late poems, there is a Yeats for every phase of our lives. He matured from somewhat gormless hawker of pretty sounds to the asker of more complex, often searing questions, not for the faint-hearted or the fey. We grow old with him, if we dare withstand the lack of comfort he offers us in his (best?) most fearful poems.

The State also grew up with Yeats, more literally: his publishing life stretched from the earnest whimsy of the Celtic Twilight 1890s, to WWII, through the Rising, the establishment of the Free State and its attendant wars, through the anxieties and identity crises of a new state establishing its ground. 'The poet', Yeats famously wrote, is '… reborn as an idea, something intended, complete'. Might the same not be said of a new State, forging a plausible and serviceable self out of origins typically messy and incoherent? Yeats was integral to that state, for all his quarrel with it. 'He invented a country', wrote Denis Donoghue, 'calling it Ireland'. It seems fitting that the final act in the forging, the Republic of Ireland Act, was signed into law on 21 December, 1948, just three months after his reburial at Drumcliffe.

Perhaps it's his public persona that has made him our National Poet? Perhaps his is the version that comes closest, historically, to what we think Irishness might mean and sound like? Or perhaps we like his distinctive music that carries even the trickiest poems so beautifully along. Or perhaps we love the work for its occasional difficulty, for the fact that some poems puzzle but still stay with us. Or for the fact that his are poems of deep feeling, not only of piercing love and desire, but also of grief, anguish, outrage, and fear. Or for his international recognition, including a Nobel Prize. Or for how quotable he is, how instantly resonant.

So many reasons to value the work. So many possible Yeats.

'National Poet': it's the kind of designation that can seal up the pleasure to be had from the poems, like a mausoleum. In undertaking to edit this special Yeats commemorative issue of *Poetry Ireland Review*, I wanted to get underneath what I termed in my letter of invitation to contributors, 'the crust of monumentalism that has accrued around Yeats'. I was hoping we could honour the poems, while throwing, perhaps, the odd and gentle water balloon at the figure of National Poet. And I was hoping to put together a lively, in earnest but entertaining issue, with nothing po-faced or stuffy about it. This was always going to involve a balancing act of respect and irreverence. Academics have filled umpteen pages with considerations of his work. Politicians have reduced him to sound bites. I wondered if there might be space between the two.

The reviews of his thirteen collections by contemporary writers were originally intended to be written from a standpoint of innocence, as if the author were reading the collection for the first time, close to its publication. I applaud those reviewers who pulled off this trick, and their essays make for what I think are forensically illuminating and fresh takes. But I also understand why not all reviewers chose to follow this approach: there is so much to be said about Yeats, he is a poet of such visceral excitement, that these reviewers wanted to engage with the collections without apparent strategy.

The new poems were commissioned with the idea of seeing where contemporary poets might walk the first line of a Yeats poem (or, in a small number of cases, a subsequent line), where it might end up. The twenty-two new poems here are by a range of Irish and (mostly) international poets: his foothold in Irish poetry is surely secure, but I also wanted to hear how his voice would sound in other accents and cadences, thrown (as it were) from other rooms.

The twenty-three essays featured offer readings and personal responses to his heritage and his poems, indicating – with humour and candour and critical insight – ways in which Yeats has influenced both the Ireland we live in, and the Ireland we read.

Thanks are due to many people, not least to our seventy contributors – the artists, writers and poets here – who have, between them, put together what I think is a response to Yeats that will matter, this year and beyond. To Laura Swift of the University of Manchester who unearthed the originals of the Yeats reviews included here. To Elizabeth Mohen, who stood guardian to the issue over her summer internship at Poetry Ireland and, as ever, to Paul Lenehan who makes of notions and proposals what we hope (as Yeats wrote in 'In Memory of Major Robert Gregory'), 'to have published all to be a world's delight'.

– Vona Groarke

Richard Murphy

REJOICE

I do not remember him then, but I must have met Michael Yeats when he came with other guests to take part in a game of cricket in one of the pastures at my grandfather's place on the Mayo-Galway borders in 1936. He was fifteen years old and I was nine. My older sister still remembers that at thirteen she was almost in love with him. Thistles and ragwort in the Pigeon Park had to be cut with a scythe to make the pitch.

I also met Michael with his wife Gráinne on a musico-literary lecture tour they were giving in Virginia in 1965. And at the Abbey Theatre in 1973, Michael generously approved my translation of the lines that Yeats had omitted from his version of Sophocles's *King Oedipus* – a kind of invisible mending I did to please Michael Cacoyannis who was directing the play at the Abbey.

My first encounter with Yeats was critically hostile. Aged seventeen, in November 1944, I was challenged in a scholarship exam for Oxford to identify the period if not the author of a wishy-washy world-weary lyric, which I guessed was written in the 1890s, and to comment on the style, which I sternly criticized. The poem, I later discovered, was 'The Sorrow of Love' in the form in which it appeared in *The Rose* (dedicated to Lionel Johnson) in 1893. In the 1930s Yeats modernized the poem, validating my critique. Here is the earlier version that I faulted:

THE SORROW OF LOVE

The quarrel of the sparrows in the eaves,
The full round moon and the star-laden sky,
And the loud song of the ever-singing leaves,
Had hid away earth's old and weary cry.

And then you came with those red mournful lips,
And with you came the whole of the world's tears,
And all the sorrows of her labouring ships,
And all the burden of her myriad years.

And now the sparrows warring in the eaves,
The crumbling moon, the white stars in the sky,
And the loud chaunting of the unquiet leaves,
Are shaken with earth's old and weary cry.

As a result of my winning the scholarship, CS Lewis became my tutor at Magdalen College. But I didn't discover Yeats – whose *Collected Poems* remained out of print throughout the 1940s – until I returned from years of schooling in England to the west of Ireland in the summer of 1946.

By chance I was invited during Galway Race week to stay in the Weir Cottage as a guest of the owner of the salmon fishery. Beside my bed, in which I was kept awake by the roar of the flowing water under my window, lay a copy of the Macmillan (London, 1940) edition of the *Last Poems and Plays* by WB Yeats, bound in green cloth. Reading these poems in the country of their birth and mine, with reverent awe that partially eclipsed understanding at the age of nineteen, at a time when the study of Eng Lit up to but not later than 1830 was beginning to pall, convinced me that I ought to look to my own mountains, lakes and waterfalls for the poetic inspiration that had eluded me in Oxford.

What impressed me more than Yeats's swaggering injunction to:

> Sing the peasantry, and then
> Hard-riding country gentlemen

was the high emblazoned rhetoric of 'The Gyres', the idea of laughter in tragic joy over the collapse of civilisation, and the sound of a voice from the cavern of ancient tombs that knows only one word, 'Rejoice!' Having survived by avoiding the horrors of the Second World War, I read this poem as gloriously prophetic and redeeming.

So I searched through desolate Connemara in that impoverished time, and found an old stone cottage without electricity or running water, but close to a river that flowed through rocks, heather and rushes. The sounds I heard were resonant with loneliness – always the wind, often the rain, sometimes a lowing cow or a braying ass. This romantic wilderness enchanted me so much that I deluded myself into believing, with the unshakeable fervour of a convert, that, if I were to listen and look and live and love with enough devotion, the words that would flow from my pen in that solitary land would be poetry.

But when I returned unwillingly to Oxford at the end of the long vacation in October 1946 – fortified by the Cuala Press 1939 edition of Yeats's *Last Poems and Two Plays*, which Mr Willie Figgis of Hodges Figgis, a friend of my father, had allowed me to buy from the glass cabinet of rare books in the back of his shop for the pre-war price of twelve shillings and six pence – the ecstasy bordering on madness induced by solitude in Connemara made me incapable of writing a weekly essay for my tutor, albeit on John Donne or George Herbert.

Now Magdalen was full of demobilised officers who had served with courage and distinction in the Second World War. To make room for these men I'd been moved out of college into dingy redbrick lodgings in a depressing time of yellow fogs and rationed food.

And when I tried to share with CS Lewis my teenage excitement in discovering Yeats, the great man said that he liked the early work but not the later. When I dared to query 'Why?', he brought the subject to an end by saying:

'Yeats was a diabolist.'

So I was lucky in meeting a brilliant, witty, widely-read law student from Belfast called Charles Monteith, whose life had been saved in the jungles of Burma by an army surgeon with whom he had shared, over a bottle of Bushmills in a tent, his love of Yeats's poetry. After a battle the next day, in which a Japanese mortar bomb had exploded at his feet, Charles was dying among the many wounded in a hospital tent when the doctor picked him out for immediate surgery.

Charles felt sympathetic to my love of Yeats and my yearning for the west of Ireland, but he thought my determination to leave Oxford in mid-term to go there to write poetry in a cottage beside a waterfall was crazy. But on the eve of my departure he gave a beer party in his rooms at which he recited from memory his favourite poems of Yeats. These became mine in the sound of his voice: 'Byzantium', 'In Memory of Eva Gore-Booth and Con Markiewicz', 'The Pilgrim', and 'The Wild Old Wicked Man'. Like Yeats, Charles was tone deaf. Music for him was unpleasant noise, but his voice carried the verbal music of those poems to my heart.

The genius of Yeats for making an unforgettable impact has also remained in my mind in Charles's plum voice and loud laughter at the end of each legendary anecdote. Once, when the dining room of the Mitre Hotel at Oxford was full of guests, according to Charles, Yeats entered in mid-conversation with a friend, declaring, 'The unsatisfactory thing about sexual intercourse is the unsoilable virginity of soul.' On another occasion, Yeats had spoken about Madame Blavatsky's experiment of levitating in an Oxford laboratory. 'And when the Professor of Physical Chemistry entered his laboratory and saw the woman lying in mid-air, he vomited.'

I began writing poetry at school in England during the war, hoping to make something that would last about the lives of people I loved. Of course Yeats did this supremely well. At a time when the economic, social and racial transformation of Ireland is obliterating more and more of the past, poetry can hold a vision of how it was or how it appeared to be. And when we have Roy Foster's magisterial two-volume life to guide us through the history, and the work of scholars such as Helen Vendler to interpret the most puzzling ideas devised by the great diabolist, the vision will remain.

Sixty-eight years ago I made my first devout pilgrimage to the places that Yeats had transfigured in the poems that meant most to me then: 'The Tower', 'Coole Park, 1929', 'Coole and Ballylee, 1931'. There was little or no traffic in the summer of 1947, and after Oranmore on the road to Gort I stopped to ask two priests or brothers the way. They had never heard of those places, not even of Kiltartan Cross.

Later I stopped to talk to an old man who was standing under a wall that he told me had been the demesne wall of Coole Park. In those days he had been chauffeur to Lady Gregory when she had no car but a carriage. At Christmas he remembered being lined up with the servants to receive presents from the mistress.

'When Mr Yeats was staying', he said, 'Lady Gregory bought presents for him to give to the staff as if from himself: but, to be sure, he couldn't recognize any of us because he was nearly blind. She had to put each present in his hand and guide him from one to the other, or he'd have had us all mixed up. And when Mr Yeats was living at the castle in Ballylee, Lady Gregory would tell me to drive over and bring him to Coole for lunch and take him back in the evening – well-fed of course.'

The ground floor of the Tower that day was mucky with the dung of a local farmer's cattle. All the furniture and woodwork had been stolen, bit by bit, because for too long, I was told, the caretaker's wages had not been paid. The winding stair remained because it was made of stone. I loved that image. Yeats's homage 'To cold Clare rock and Galway rock and thorn', in his elegy for Major Robert Gregory, thrilled me. I felt it secretly validated my revolting determination to write poetry in spite of being born in a demesne house with military ancestors going back to the conquests of Cromwell and Queen Elizabeth.

Yeats as a visionary had no real contact with the soil, but my Murphy ancestors from Carlow had little else. Having turned into great poetry his passion for the mystery and beauty of lakes, woods and hills in his own parts of Galway and Sligo, Yeats had left me just enough space to write about the sea and the life of northwest Connemara and its islands where I lived for more than twenty years – Cleggan, Inishbofin, Omey and High Island.

It seems fitting that the author of *A Vision* had defective eyesight. Wasn't Homer blind, blind as a bat? As for me, I never saw a ghost on the lime-tree avenue of my birthplace, nor could I suspend my disbelief in magic or in the occult or in God after the age of nineteen. In the gloom of post-war Oxford, brilliant scepticism, logical positivism, and irony pre-vailed, with disregard or disdain for CS Lewis.

As a child, I loved the sound 'of clay and wattles made' without knowing what those words meant. Now, near the end of a long life two oceans away from 'Innisfree', in a garden of spices, tea and gold king coconuts, and in a world that has changed utterly, I've watched men build little walls of wet clay on a frame of bamboo wattles. Knowing the clay was trodden by buffaloes increases my pleasure in observing the practice of an ancient craft that underlies the sonority of an ideal in Yeats's poem. Things have often interested me more than the ideas they represent in poetry. Sometimes I have erred in being too literal or too low key.

'What thou lovest well remains, the rest is dross.' The poetry of Yeats, which I still love well, remains to lighten my darkness. Today, my friends in resplendent Sri Lanka are finishing a small coconut palm-roofed hexagon with those half-high clay and wattle walls, and an earthen floor coated with fresh cow-dung. There I will go and sit in our garden thinking, if and when I can, 'Of what is past, or passing, or to come'.

Part of this essay is an abridged version of Richard Murphy's address at the opening of the 2007 Yeats International Summer School.

Tessa Hadley

BODIES BLESSED

On the flyleaf of my Macmillan *Complete Poems* I have written 'Tessa
Nichols, 1976', which means that I bought it when I was twenty and at
university. The poems came first, before I was able to fit around them
any knowledge of Irish history, or of the writer and his context. First of
all, of course, I responded to the music: I couldn't resist 'The silver
apples of the moon, / The golden apples of the sun'. Because I was
trying to teach myself to judge literature like FR Leavis, I knew it was a
dangerous seduction and they were the wrong kind of apples; luckily
I've never been susceptible to any guilt about reading, I've always read
what I loved. Leavis was as ineffectual, warning against seduction, as any
vicar or maiden aunt. He said it was repulsive to 'lie down where all the
ladders start / In the foul rag and bone shop of the heart', but I
recognized the place and the pessimism – it didn't even seem to me like
pessimism, I was too interested in all the rags and bones.

When I came to read the poems more consecutively, I recognized
how the sweet yearning of the early music changed around the end of
the first decade of the century, when Yeats was in his forties. Some force
of thought begins to intrude against the grain of the verse, a gritty friction
that's like a resistance in the material itself. There's a new contemporaneity,
and its plain speech is counteractive to the music's seduction, thereby
strengthening and deepening it. In place of a plangent dying fall in the
sound ('Sweetheart, do not love too long'), there's a masterly reiterative
stutter and swagger which mimes the reader's excitement, stumbling into
the thought ('Suddenly I saw the cold and rook-delighting heaven / That
seemed as though ice burned and was but the more ice'). The poems'
lexicon breaks out of the mythic frame, too, but doesn't leave it behind,
only wrenches and develops it, so that the poems can accommodate
coffee cups and aeroplanes now alongside the gyres and Queens and 'the
symbolic rose'. When his ghosts go naked out onto the road, they are
our ghosts, or our contemporaries'. He's driving his mythic paradigms
inside modernity, or reimagining modernity around those paradigms.
Something in his genius, combined with the special conditions obtaining
in Ireland at that time, made it possible for him to be, consummately and
in the same gesture, a great Romantic poet and also a twentieth-century
modernist. (FR Leavis says something like this, doesn't he? So he wasn't
all wrong).

One reason Yeats speaks to me may be because I've found in his
poems the satisfactions that novels give: rich elements of narrative and

argument, not hidden but eloquently explicit. I like this obviousness out on the surface, this naming of big things: the compromise of politics, the argument between doubt and commitment, regret for wasted opportunity, hopeless love, recognitions that come too late. Eventually I learned more about Yeats's world and his life, and read Foster's marvellous biography; all that monumental grand-gesture living, and belonging to an age in a particular place, and trying to seize it and shape its public life, hardly seemed something separate from the poetry – for once, the life and the writing are one story. It's extraordinary that the public life doesn't take its toll on the freedom, the audacious leap, of the poetry, but it doesn't.

I've never for one moment been tempted by, or even interested in, the esoterica, The Golden Dawn and so on. If it's interesting that he and George spend their honeymoon doing automatic writing, that's only because it's such a funny, telling story – she was just managing him, wasn't she? Managing his panic and tidying away the foolish misjudged yearning for Iseult. It's difficult in our era, to make sense of all that proliferation of mysticisms about the turn of the last century: it all smells so fake and stuffy to us – the long faces and Gilbert and Sullivan theatricals. Yet the very same material, transmuted into poetic form, commands me in the poems, with all the momentousness of the great religious languages.

They ran something by Yeats on the tube a little while ago, as part of the inspired and life-saving Poems on the Underground. I thought at first it was a new short poem I didn't know – actually it's part, surely the best part, of something longer ('Vacillation').

> My fiftieth year had come and gone,
> I sat, a solitary man,
> In a crowded London shop,
> An open book and empty cup
> On the marble table-top.
>
> While on the shop and street I gazed
> My body of a sudden blazed;
> And twenty minutes more or less
> It seemed, so great my happiness,
> That I was blessed and could bless.

I read it on my way to London shops, and it was as if the same miracle of electric insight that Yeats described leaped out from the words on the advertising board and across the carriage – that mysterious transformative power, the power of art to make us blessed, to pass on blessings between man and man, or man and woman.

Sheenagh Pugh

THE SWAIN STAGE

WB Yeats, *Crossways* (1889).

Here we have a slim volume (sixteen poems) by a new, young voice, and
as is only natural, we hear in it many and diverse influences from his
reading. In the juxtaposition of the 'Happy' and 'Sad' Shepherds, we may
fancy echoes of Milton's 'L'Allegro' and 'Il Penseroso', though the actual
language and spirit of both are more reminiscent of the Pre-Raphaelites.
In his songs and ballads, he is influenced by the folk-song and folk-tale of
his native Ireland. The little group of 'Indian' poems is something else
again; they do not, to me, read like the work of anyone who has ever set
foot in India, but are clearly by someone who has read and thought
much about it.

Mr Yeats is technically accomplished beyond what might be expected
of a poet still in his mid-twenties; his handling of rhyme, metre and a
variety of verse forms cannot be faulted and in his more song-like poems
like 'Down by the Salley Gardens', he shows a very musical ear. This
poem, indeed, has not only the movement but some of the archetypal
feel of genuine folk-song. One can well imagine it set to music and sung.

His use of language is less consistent in quality. At times in his more
formal poems, especially when he is speaking of some abstraction, he
can sound rather flat and vapid:

> 'I make the cloak of Sorrow:
> O lovely to see in all men's sight
> Shall be the cloak of Sorrow,
> In all men's sight.'
> – 'THE CLOAK, THE BOAT, AND THE SHOES'

His 'Shepherd' pieces, metrically flawless as they are, sound sometimes
uninvolved, more like exercises in a form than anything the poet truly
needed to write. And his dialogue pieces often sound like no kind of
conversation that ever was or could be uttered by a human being.
Admittedly, Mr Yeats is not aiming for the naturalism of, say, a Browning,
but there is a difference between elevated and unbelievable. There is a
striking change in the quality of the language in 'Ephemera', which
begins with two people conversing, if one can call it that, about the fact
that their love is waning (and if they frequently address each other in
terms like 'When the poor tired child, Passion, falls asleep' and 'Passion

has often worn our wandering hearts', one can see why). But then the poet's attention turns to the surroundings of these fluent conversationalists, and all of a sudden the artificiality quite disappears:

> The woods were round them, and the yellow leaves
> Fell like faint meteors in the gloom, and once
> A rabbit old and lame limped down the path;
> Autumn was over him ...

That rabbit is instantly believable and alive, and worth ten of the high-flown, contrived lines that preceded him. And how striking and memorable that image of the leaves as 'faint meteors'! Here we have pure, sharp observation, transmuted by language that looks simple but in which each word has been carefully chosen. To some degree, this happens too in 'The Stolen Child', again where he is evoking the natural world he knows. As long as we are watching the 'flapping herons', or 'brown mice bob / Round and round the oatmeal-chest', the landscape and the poem itself live: it is marred, to my ear, by some utterly predictable feminine rhymes (berries / cherries, bubbles / troubles), and to some extent too by comparison with what was surely its inspiration, Mr Allingham's famous 'The Faeries'. The poems share not only their subject matter, the old belief that fairies steal away human children, but even the reference to the landmark, the Rosses. But Mr Allingham's poem, though superficially gayer and certainly easier to sing, is at bottom darker: his stolen child is explicitly dead, while 'The Stolen Child' here ends by going off with the fairies; there are hints, indeed, in the last verse that he has been lured away from domestic safety, but the refrain 'From a world more full of weeping than he can understand' may suggest something better in prospect. I find myself uneasy with this romantic view of the matter; if we are to have fairies in poetry at all, so late in the nineteenth century, I think I should prefer Mr Allingham's unsentimental view of them as cruel, frivolous and amoral.

That Mr Yeats can also write credible dialogue, when he chooses, is evident from one of his ballad pieces. There are three poems in this metre, and I do not find 'The Ballad of Father O'Hart' and 'The Ballad of the Foxhunter' particularly successful. The latter, about an old hunting man's death being mourned by his hounds, is marred by sentimentality; the former perhaps depends too much on a knowledge of its context, but even having ascertained the meanings of 'shoneen' and 'sleiveen', I was left in some doubt as to what the poet intended by the ending. But in the third, 'The Ballad of Moll Magee', a first-person piece, he creates a most credible and moving voice for an old woman teased by small children. She tells her sad story (exhausted by her work salting herring all day, she fatally 'overlays' her baby and is turned out by her husband) in a matter-of-fact way that is more affecting than sentimentality could ever be:

> A weary woman sleeps so hard!
> My man grew red and pale,
> And gave me money, and bade me go
> To my own place, Kinsale.

> He drove me out and shut the door,
> And gave his curse to me;
> I went away in silence,
> No neighbour could I see.

> The windows and the doors were shut,
> One star shone faint and green,
> The little straws were turnin' round
> Across the bare boreen.

Again we see the acute observation of the natural world, which always seems to sharpen this poet's language. I cannot help thinking that the 'Indian' poems, though they are not without interest, are less memorable in their language precisely because they are not set in the landscape with which this poet is familiar and in which he finds inspiration.

In 'The Meditation of the Old Fisherman' too, we hear intermittently a very believable voice, and also the use of refrain that is so often part of this poet's musicality:

> You waves, though you dance by my feet like children at play,
> Though you glow and you glance, though you purr and you dart;
> In the Junes that were warmer than these are, the waves were more gay,
> *When I was a boy with never a crack in my heart.*

> The herring are not in the tides as they were of old;
> My sorrow! for many a creak gave the creel in the cart
> That carried the take to Sligo town to be sold,
> *When I was a boy with never a crack in my heart.*

It is not easy to see where this young poet will go next, for it is already clear that he has not one 'voice' but several. I should say, unhesitatingly, that the most successful pieces in this short volume were those in the voices of plain, simple people rather than over-fluent talkers, those that give free rein to the poet's musicality rather than those that confine him in iambic or trochaic couplets, and those that are rooted in the countryside he sees so acutely. But that does not necessarily mean he will, or should, confine himself to those paths: a young poet properly has many ambitions and wishes not only to do what he can already do well but to branch out into what he has not yet mastered. He clearly has, for instance, a great liking for dialogue and will surely attempt more in that form (though one hopes his protagonists will not continue to talk like slightly pompous and self-absorbed professors), while some of his Indian poems indicate an interest in philosophical and religious questions that has not, so far, surfaced in his other work. Myself I should like to hear more of people like Moll and the fisherman, and rather less of the kind of self-pitying lovesick swain who parts from his sweetheart 'With a kiss and a tear on thy drooping brow' at the end of 'The Falling of the Leaves', a poem which reads so curiously like an early draft for 'Ephemera' that I think it ought perhaps to have been omitted from the collection. But perhaps lovesick swains are a stage a young poet must go through. It is more remarkable that he should, at this age, have been able to succeed at bringing alive Moll, the fisherman and that rabbit.

Note: Most of the poems now collected under the title of *Crossways* were originally published in *The Wanderings of Oisin and Other Poems* (Kegan Paul, Trench & Co, 1889).

WB Yeats

FRIENDS

Now must I these three praise –
Three women that have wrought
What joy is in my days:
One because no thought,
Nor those unpassing cares,
No, not in these fifteen
Many-times-troubled years,
Could ever come between
Mind and delighted mind;
And one because her hand
Had strength that could unbind
What none can understand,
What none can have and thrive,
Youth's dreamy load, till she
So changed me that I live
Labouring in ecstasy.
And what of her that took
All till my youth was gone
With scarce a pitying look?
How could I praise that one?
When day begins to break
I count my good and bad,
Being wakeful for her sake,
Remembering what she had,
What eagle look still shows,
While up from my heart's root
So great a sweetness flows
I shake from head to foot.

August Kleinzahler

APRIL, 1920

Now I must these three praise –
Po'boys, gumbo, crawfish etouffeé.
It's a long ocean voyage away, indeed,
From mackerel, champ and day old disheen.
They griped in Waco: 'He's over our heads.'
Probably so ... Some things best left unsaid.
Americans, on balance, seem an amiable people,
If all about commerce, sports and steeples.
The Crescent City is quite another place.
You'd hardly know you were in the United States.
French, black, Creole, redneck, what have you.
It all makes for good craic down on the bayou.
I was once of the opinion that Maud was red hot
But she never had a quarter of what these gals got.
Georgie's upstairs with her mystic scribbling.
I'm here in the bar downstairs, reconsidering
The manner in which my life has been spent
Fashioning verses in lieu of merriment.
Perhaps it's only the 3 sazeracs talking
But give me tuba / drums / cornet over gyre-stalking.
A pity, tomorrow we'll be on our way
Just when I was ready to *laissez les bon temps rouler.*

WB Yeats

THE NINETEENTH CENTURY AND AFTER

Though the great song return no more
There's keen delight in what we have:
The rattle of pebbles on the shore
Under the receding wave.

Heather McHugh

Though *the great song* return no more
In air or folio, we're less
Demanding of it, in our
Anger ghettos. (Agent got hers,

Then got rages.) Meterless?
Get thee with metronome. No flow
Of cursives from your quill? Get Arial.
(Relaxatives for happiness.)

Go gather tens where hundreds wilt:
All meanings are in store.
In stock, in fact. In home décor.
(Love it to list it: beds atilt

Towards the Candy-cam.) And when
Her *anger gets hot, gags the tenor,*
Let the yester-jig be done.
Tomorrow's tiny ticker runs

On enemas and anagrams.

Colm Tóibín

POEM AND SHADOW

Some of his poems have shadow poems. It was as though in his argument with himself he had sometimes been too loud or declarative, too much a man performing, and now in the shadow poem he is alone. Daylight has been replaced by lamplight, noise by silence, the speaking voice by the voice whispering, many listeners by one single attentive presence. In some poems the emotion is too raw or unformed; the will was there, however, and the impulse was pressing and serious, but the impulse was not enough or was too much. In any case, there are times when Yeats's poems come in pairs and, while the first is all flourish and finish, fully assured, magisterial, the second is mysterious, tentative or oddly fragile and personal.

One of the best examples of the tonal distance and the thematic connection between two poems is 'September 1913' and 'The Fisherman'. The first poem addresses a crowd. It is full of questions, but they are all rhetorical; it is full of emotion, but much of it is contained anger and open contempt. The poem is ready to use refrain and proclamation as though something patently and obviously true were being stated. 'The Fisherman', on the other hand, is filled with suggestion rather than state-ment. While 'September 1913' uses iambic tetrameter with all its clanging certainties, 'The Fisherman' uses an iambic trimeter, which is closer to a soft voice speaking, and which varies in the last three lines, allowing in a sense of sudden understanding or determination against the soft-edged sound of the lines that come before.

There is every difference between the very first line of the two poems – 'What need you being come to sense' and 'Although I can see him still', the first line arrogant and challenging, the second exploratory and directed inwards. 'The Fisherman' lets dream and the process of personal vision itself into the poem, but it deals, in fact, with the same drama as 'September 1913', which is the conflict between philistinism, public and private, and the life of the spirit, or the life of the imagination. Both poems exalt the idea of art; they privilege complexity against vulgarity, greed and stark simplicity against the common and the clever.

A further example of two poems on the same theme is provided by two of Yeats's responses to the death of Robert Gregory – 'In Memory of Major Robert Gregory' and 'An Irish Airman Foresees His Death'. Once more, the first poem uses a longer line and a regular stanza form – the form of the poem is based on the seventeenth-century poet Abraham

Cowley's 'Ode on the Death of Mr William Hervey'. The second poem, as with 'The Fisherman', does not have stanza breaks and is written in the first person singular. While 'In Memory of Major Robert Gregory' is written in the first personal singular too, it is addressed to a public as though on a ceremonial occasion.

'In Memory of Major Robert Gregory' has an aura of a poem of pure finish, with certainty in the rhymes and in the stanza forms, with a particular polish and finality in the last line of each eight-line stanza. It is a poem that invokes heroism and manly perfection, and combines this with a strange underlying emotion as Gregory is named only in the title and not referred to at all in the body of the poem until the sixth stanza. Yeats manages to match a tone in the poem filled with high, idealized suggestions and statements with another tone that is awed and bowed down by the death of his friend's son. Thus the public sound of the poem has an undertone of private feeling.

Just as in 'The Fisherman', in which Yeats inhabits his dream-self, creating a private voice, now in 'An Irish Airman Foresees His Death' Yeats creates a dream self too, this time a voice speaking from the dead. It is as though, in hushed cadences, Robert Gregory is replying to the grandiose claims made for him in the other more highly-wrought poem, as though he is dealing in a way which is placid and almost comforting with the idea, at the end of 'In Memory of Major Robert Gregory', that his death, for Yeats, 'took all my heart for speech'.

This is, then, a poem of pure speech. The first line has eight words, each of one syllable only. The voice will not be filled with flourishes, but with raw and uneasy truth; the epigrammatic lines and use of paradox seem natural and hard-won, mined from experience rather than contrived for a poem. As in 'The Fisherman', the poem lists the people or things of which it disapproves, who seem inimical to the very tone the poem is attempting to create. In this poem, it is:

> Nor law, nor duty bade me fight,
> Nor public men, nor cheering crowds ...

In 'The Fisherman', the enemies are listed as:

> The craven man in his seat,
> The insolent unreproved,
> And no knave brought to book
> Who has won a drunken cheer,
> The witty man and his joke
> Aimed at the commonest ear,
> The clever man who cries
> The catch-cries of the clown ...

These two poems seek to create a space for spiritual autonomy, for the idea of the solitary soul and the notion that speech-in-dream and speech-in-death can combine both a simplicity and a complexity not available to most, and indeed anathema to those listed in the poem as the enemies. Even though there is a sense of isolated splendour in the voices, Yeats is careful in these two poems not to exalt the speaker but to offer him a humility that in turn leads to a stark truth and eloquence.

Two other poems that seem to echo each other, or indeed reply to each other, are 'Sailing to Byzantium' and 'Byzantium'. The country in the opening of the first poem is a real place, the season is summer; there is a sense of real light, daylight. In 'Byzantium', on the other hand, it is night in a place that may have been imagined as much as seen, and is invoked as much as described. In the first, death is related to ageing and to decay; the body is almost the enemy of the soul. In the second, death is a form of energy, mirrored in the fierce energy of the poem's own diction.

The world of 'Byzantium' is, like the world of 'The Fisherman' and of 'An Irish Airman Foresees His Death', a dream world that allows, nonetheless, great clarity of vision, moments of pure distinction and sudden realization.

The poem dramatizes in ghostly sounds the human spirit at its most desolate and grand and exalted. The power of its play between light and darkness, its forceful insistence on death as action, depend on the poem's high-toned music. The constant repetition, the certainty in the hard iambic beat in some of the lines, the insistence of taking the most abstract terms and phrases and making them seem real and concrete and true, add gravity and strangeness to the poem's magisterial weight.

Both 'Sailing to Byzantium' and 'Byzantium' deal with time and eternity, energy and beauty, art and image. Both poems insist on a heightened tension between what is visible and mortal and what will outlast the body and its time. Both poems insist also on the importance of soul, the ineffable; they attempt to offer substance and shape to what will outlive mortal time. The first poem, written in iambic pentameter, has four stanzas of eight lines and the rhyme scheme is *abababcc* which gives the last couplet the kind of certainty and completion which was achieved using other means in 'September 1913' (which has a refrain) and 'In Memory of Major Robert Gregory' (where the last line of each stanza is longer than the line before it).

The opening stanza of 'Byzantium' has great metric variation, using a sound-base which is iambic pentameter, but using also lines of two and three beats mid-stanza, like drum sounds, or bell sounds, before a final line in each of the five stanzas which has five clear ringing beats. The poem's rhyme scheme is complex, being *aacddc*.

While 'Sailing to Byzantium' sees the real world and then imagines the spirit, for 'Byzantium', the exploratory, ghostly and tentative cadences attempt to establish a realm for the spirit itself; the realm is made close, it seems inhabited, it is filled with mysterious ritual, but it is filled also with a sense of things which have been observed, examined and are made real, rather than merely imagined in the poem's ghostly-sounding procedures. 'Byzantium' offers energy and an aura of reality to a world that may have been dreamed into being but has, courtesy of the poem's diction, been made all the more present for that. So, too, in the other echo poems, such as 'The Fisherman' and 'An Irish Airman Foresees His Death', the fragile voice, the voice from a dream or from death, is given palpability, is allowed its own strangeness, its own mysterious force in opposition to more public poems, poems of certainty that were inspired by the same material, the same arguments.

Vijay Seshadri

MICROTONES

Probably because there were almost no points of contact, external or
internal, between Yeats's experience and my own – even his enthusiasm
for India, where I was born, seemed already to me, at the age of sixteen,
as obviously, and obliviously, far-fetched as Herman Hesse's – he taught
me more than anyone else about poetry in the years when I was first
reading poems seriously. His subject matter wasn't exactly incidental to
the pleasure I got from him, but it was improbable enough, even though
it was often political, to a teenager living in the American Midwest
during Vietnam and the civil-rights movement, and in the rising tide of
second-wave feminism. His feelings and allegiances were just as distant.
At the same time, though, his language was immediate and stirring, and
his voice was recognizable because he was a major, often unacknowledged,
influence on that whole generation of contemporary American poets –
black and white – I was reading as I encountered him. This helped me to
distinguish, much more sharply than through those poets – whose
interior and exterior landscapes were closer to my own – the variable
(subject matter, landscape, and, in fact, feeling) in poetry from the fixed
(rhetorical, syntactic, and lexical verve; metaphorical power; musical
invention and balance; dynamics; sentence sound, as Frost called it;
athletic movement; formal judiciousness and grace; timing and surprise).
The relationship between form and representation is harder to account
for in language arts than it is in visual arts or music, as is the way in
which that relationship contributes to our enjoyment, but Yeats was the
first poet who taught me that it was, in fact, the relationship itself, and
not the one thing or the other, that defined poetry. It seems a little
strange to say it, but Yeats taught me how to read Ashbery far better than
artists who came from Ashbery's milieu and shared his project.

I wasn't cold to all of Yeats's content. The Maud Gonne stuff was
embarrassing (I found it even more embarrassing when I read years later
about the actual details of that relationship). But I couldn't get enough of
miraculous inner shapes like this one, and the romance they implied ...

> The light of evening, Lissadell,
> Great windows open to the south,
> Two girls in silk kimonos, both
> Beautiful, one a gazelle

... even though they sprang from the same place in the poet's psyche as
his unfortunate infatuations. The valetudinarianism was hard to

empathize with then (not anymore). I didn't get 'A terrible beauty is born' (really?), but I understood the distinction of the plain-spoken gravity of the poem that houses that line. And about the feudal Mrs French's serving man – who anticipated his mistress's wishes so completely that he brought her 'in a little covered dish' the ears of a farmer who had been insolent to her, which he had clipped off with the garden shears – I was outraged and disgusted, but didn't feel the need to deny myself the magnificence of the rest of that poem, 'The Tower'.

I was receptive to impressions at sixteen, but that probably doesn't sufficiently explain why Yeats's poems inscribed themselves automatically on my brain at that age. I never memorized him actively, like I later did other poets I got attached to, but there are passages and whole poems, couplets and quatrains amounting to hundreds of lines flocking around in my head. 'Crazy Jane Grown Old Looks at the Dancers'; 'Why Should Not Old Men Be Mad?'; 'I summon to the winding ancient stair; / Set all your mind upon the steep ascent, / Upon the broken, crumbling battlement, / Upon the breathless starlit air, / Upon the star that marks the hidden pole; / Fix every wandering thought upon / That quarter where all thought is done: / Who can distinguish darkness from the soul?'

Yeats still has the same freshness in my mind. Hardy and Auden and Frost, Bishop and Lowell, sound like themselves, and reveal through their tones their culture and period. Yeats, for some hard-to-fully-explain reasons, sounds like me, like all of us, and that is neither illusion nor delusion. Maybe it is because his line is never slack, the intonations are flawless, the stresses are never uncertain, the internal balance of the line is always maintained – their character never descends into personality, so nothing impure enters his diction, nothing at the cellular level of the poem is overly marked by history, by an identity that isn't absolutely individual. He seems as limpid as Ella Fitzgerald, and at that level of perfect clarity in performance. In the poems of the period from the volume *Responsibilities* onward, the conversational tones and microtones have such accuracy and precision that they travel across historical periods. Another reason, maybe, that he never sounds dated to me is also relational, as in the relationship between form and content, rather than substantial. The tone is conversational but the diction is elevated with an exquisite tension ever so slightly above the conversational, and the relation between the natural tone and the subtly elevated diction, the bristling energy between them, establishes a sonic order that seems untarnished by time.

Yeats has been criticized for his music (a word that is shorthand in poetry for disparate elements): Larkin said that it was like garlic, it got into everything. Pound dismissed what he considered its narrow range by saying that his former employer would just get a 'chune' in his head, as if his control of sonic effects were merely percussive and primitively melodic. A visitor to his parlour heard the poet pacing and humming in the room overhead and was told by Mrs Yeats that that was just Willie buzzing like a bumble-bee.

They were, as far as my ear can tell, all just jealous.

Colette Bryce

GONNE GIRL

William Butler Yeats, *The Rose* (1893).

> *Come near; I would, before my time to go,*
> *Sing of old Eire and the ancient ways:*
> *Red Rose, proud Rose, sad Rose of all my days.*
>   − 'TO THE ROSE UPON THE ROOD OF TIME'

The symbol of the rose is a flexible one for the young Yeats in this, his second collection of lyrics, encompassing the Róisín Dubh of Irish history, romantic love, nationalist sacrifice, and eternal beauty. Epitomizing the ideal of eternal beauty 'wandering on her way' is the figure of Maud Gonne − in life a tireless political activist, and in the poems of *The Rose* the subject of a series of lyrics on irreconcilable love.

'When You Are Old', the most famous of these, portrays a woman ravaged by age and close to death. Full of regrets, she must comfort herself by reading the very poem that has rendered her thus:

> When you are old and grey and full of sleep,
> And nodding by the fire, take down this book,
> And slowly read, and dream of the soft look
> Your eyes had once, and of their shadows deep ...

It is one of the poems that comes to mind when considering Adrienne Rich's idea of 're-vision', seeing a familiar text afresh in terms of male depictions of women. As Rich noted, '[The] women [in the poems] were almost always beautiful, but threatened with the loss of beauty, the loss of youth − the fate worse than death. Or, they were beautiful and died young ... Or, the woman was like Maud Gonne, cruel and disastrously mistaken, and the poem reproached her because she had refused to become a luxury for the poet.'[*]

Today we are a little over-informed about Yeats's ardour for Maud Gonne, later redirected at her daughter. It adds to a romantic myth around the poet, the floppy fringe of hopeless devotion, a 'Gonne or none' paralysis leading to the biographical embarrassment of prolonged virginity. That these early lyrics deal more in a capitalized notion of 'Love' than actual relationships is, on the other hand, to be expected in their post Pre-Raphaelite shade.

Loss of physical beauty is again threatened in 'The Two Trees' with its repeated 'Gaze no more in the bitter glass'; and troubling as the psychology of the fireside scene might seem in 'When You Are Old', a darker note is sounded in 'A Dream of Death':

> I dreamed that one had died in a strange place
> Near no accustomed hand;
> And they had nailed the boards over her face,
> The peasants of that land ...

The vision is again bound up with the poet's literary immortality, a kind of deathly version of the rescue fantasy – the rescue not of the woman herself but of her memory, through the poet's words.

> And left her to the indifferent stars above
> Until I carved these words:
> *She was more beautiful than thy first love,*
> *But now lies under boards.*

In 'The Countess Cathleen in Paradise', the eponymous heroine is consigned, inevitably, to the 'oaken press' (via the printing press). The word 'mournful' is repeatedly attributed to Gonne, 'mournful beauty', 'mournful lips', 'mournful pride', even as the poems act out a desire to mourn *her*; as poet-mourner, the problem of unrequited sexual desire might be dispensed with once and for all. Gonne is known to have encouraged Yeats's love poems, hand in hand with rejecting his proposals, and it's ironic that her posthumous fame is indeed greatest between the 'boards' of his many biographies. At an interesting angle to the above tropes, we find an attempt to escape the body through a kind of willow pattern metamorphosis:

> I would that we were, my beloved, white birds on the foam of the sea!
> We tire of the flame of the meteor, before it can fade and flee ...
> — 'THE WHITE BIRDS'

'The Lake Isle of Innisfree' makes a quiet debut, innocent as yet of a gift-shop ubiquity that will come to rival the Serenity Prayer. The young Yeats considered it his first poem 'with anything in its rhythm of my own music' and he was right; the effects are wonderfully acoustic, calling up emotion in the reader through unexpected rhythmic substitutions and subtle consonantal chains. The marriage of musicality with an uncharacteristically direct speaking voice points forward to the great lyrics of his middle period. At this point, the reader might be relieved to read of such things as bean-rows and pavements from a poet so generally drawn to the mystical symbol and grand statement. The poem remains one of the great London poems, giving voice to the peculiar intensified nostalgia – for the natural world as much as home ground – experienced by the Irish emigrants swallowed up by that city.

Elsewhere, the poet sets out his Revival stall on Irish folklore, to 'Sing of old Eire and the ancient ways', with uneven results. Among the highs are these closing lines from 'Fergus and the Druid':

> I see my life go drifting like a river
> From change to change; I have been many things –
> A green drop in the surge, a gleam of light
> Upon a sword, a fir-tree on a hill,
> An old slave grinding at a heavy quern,
> A king sitting upon a chair of gold –
> And all these things were wonderful and great;
> But now I have grown nothing, knowing all.
> Ah! Druid, Druid, how great webs of sorrow
> Lay hidden in the small slate-coloured thing!

Less successful in this vein are several verse narratives which don't quite achieve lift off, 'The Man Who Dreamed of Faeryland' for example, or 'The Ballad of Father Gilligan'. An ambitious retelling of 'Cuchulain's Fight with the Sea', an alluring subject for the young poet in terms of his own filial anxieties, rather fails to flow, partly as a result of ungrounded dialogue. This aspect of the collection earned Yeats one of his least appreciative reviews, in *The Illustrated London News,* from a baffled William Watson:

> To supplement his human puppets – we cannot say his human beings,
> for being they have none, in the sense of life or life-likeness – he invokes
> the aid of all manner of supernatural and elemental agencies, spirits and
> fairies, and what not, together with sowlths and tevishes, whatever they
> may be, for we unblushingly confess our ignorance of their nature or
> attributes.

But how do the poems sound today, played on the contemporary jukebox? Wistful, lilting. A little Oirish? Sometimes. Unmistakably Early Yeats and thus out of sync, as they ought to be, with our post-postmodern settings. Flashes of brilliance alert us to what is to come.

The Rose concludes with a rousing apologia 'To Ireland in the Coming Times', which seeks to defend the collection from being underrated due to its focus on a woman, one whose *'red-rose-bordered hem* [...] *Trails all about the written page'*. The ideal reader is left in no doubt about the poet's estimation of his own, and the book's, importance.

Nor may I less be counted one
With Davis, Mangan, Ferguson,
Because, to him who ponders well,
My rhymes more than their rhyming tell
Of things discovered in the deep,
Where only body's laid asleep.

*Adrienne Rich, *On Lies, Secrets, and Silence: Selected Prose 1966-1978*

Note: *The Rose* is the title of a section of Yeats's collected poems selected (except for 'Who Goes with Fergus?' and 'To Some I have Talked with by the Fire', added to *The Rose* in later printings) from *The Countess Kathleen and Various Legends and Lyrics* (T. Fisher Unwin, 1892).

WB Yeats

HOUND VOICE

Because we love bare hills and stunted trees
And were the last to choose the settled ground,
Its boredom of the desk or of the spade, because
So many years companioned by a hound,
Our voices carry; and though slumber-bound,
Some few half wake and half renew their choice,
Give tongue, proclaim their hidden name – 'hound voice'.

The women that I picked spoke sweet and low
And yet gave tongue. 'Hound voices' were they all.
We picked each other from afar and knew
What hour of terror comes to test the soul,
And in that terror's name obeyed the call,
And understood, what none have understood,
Those images that waken in the blood.

Some day we shall get up before the dawn
And find our ancient hounds before the door,
And wide awake know that the hunt is on;
Stumbling upon the blood-dark track once more,
Then stumbling to the kill beside the shore;
Then cleaning out and bandaging of wounds,
And chants of victory amid the encircling hounds.

Margaret Atwood

BECAUSE WE LOVE BARE HILLS AND STUNTED TREES

Because we love bare hills and stunted trees
we head north when we can,
past taiga, tundra, rocky shoreline, ice.

Where does it come from, this sparse taste
of ours? How long
did we roam this hardscape, learning by heart
all that we used to know:
turn skin fur side in,
partner with wolves, eat fat, hate waste,
carve spirit, respect the snow,
build and guard flame?

Everything once had a soul,
even this clam, this pebble.
Each had a secret name.
Everything listened.
Everything was real,
but didn't always love you.
You needed to take care.

We long to go back there,
or so we like to feel
when it's not too cold.
We long to pay that much attention.
But we've lost the knack;
also there's other music.
All we hear in the wind's plainsong
is the wind.

WB Yeats

THE MUSICIANS

I

(*singing*) At the grey round of the hill
Music of a lost kingdom
Runs, runs and is suddenly still.
The winds out of Clare-Galway
Carry it: suddenly it is still.

I have heard in the night air
A wandering airy music;
And moidered in that snare
A man is lost of a sudden,
In that sweet wandering snare.

What finger first began
Music of a lost kingdom?
They dreamed that laughed in the sun.
Dry bones that dream are bitter,
They dream and darken our sun.

Those crazy fingers play
A wandering airy music;
Our luck is withered away,
And wheat in the wheat-ear withered,
And the wind blows it away.

II

My heart ran wild when it heard
The curlew cry before dawn
And the eddying cat-headed bird;
But now the night is gone.
I have heard from far below
The strong March birds a-crow,
Stretch neck and clap the wing,
Red cocks, and crow.

Adam Thorpe

BY SILBURY

At the grey round of the hill
I walk in the snares of grass
By thistles as tall as me: the hill
Is herself. Between us, however, a barbed-
Wire fence gathers its wool.

I stop to take a photograph
And no number of these will snare
The music of the hill. My photograph
Dreams in its little machine:
Little coloured ghost of a photograph.

The world slips so easily away.
The thistle nods its heavy load.
The hooves have printed the bridleway.
I carry about with me a myriad of ghosts
And the hill knows they are running away.

The hill knows they are running like cows
At the sound of a gate through the evening air:
At the foot of her slope are the tiny cows
Stilled like a painting in the morning calm
While the stream-side oaks spray whorls of crows.

A CONVERSATION WITH ROY FOSTER, YEATS BIOGRAPHER,
AND VONA GROARKE

VG You published *The Arch Poet*, the second part of your Yeats biography, in 2003. Does WBY still occupy your thoughts to any significant extent, or is that project well and truly complete?

RF George Moore said 'Everything begins in Yeats and ends in Yeats' and for me he is still, as he himself said of Swift, around every corner. The biography took 18 years to research and write and is full and comprehensive but there are always grace notes that one would like to add, and subjects which I think I could have spent more time on – his plays, for instance. Above all Yeats's eerie sense of the future means that his ideas about history and destiny have an abiding interest still. In a subsequent book, *Words Alone: Yeats and his Inheritances*, based on the Clark Lectures which I gave at Cambridge in 2009, I went back and looked at his early work in the light of what he was 'inheriting' from his predecessors and contemporaries, rather than seeing him principally as a great innovator; and I felt there really was something new to say here, in addition to what I'd put down in print already.

VG You're an historian, but did an interest in WBY's poems inform your decision to take on the biography at all?

RF Absolutely. My mother (who was an English teacher) went to school in Sligo and adored Yeats and read us the poems (the simpler ones!) as children; I still remember her reading 'The Fiddler of Dooney' and after the lines 'For the good are always the merry, / Save by an evil chance'. remarking reflectively: 'Yes – there's always that *evil chance*.' And much later, when I was studying history at Trinity, I read Conor Cruise O'Brien's *Parnell and his Party*, and I was very struck by the way he used Yeats's poetry to illuminate Parnell's charismatic aura and the mystique which continued after his death. Later, hearing Leland Lyons's Ford Lectures at Oxford (which became the book *Culture and Anarchy in Ireland*), I was excited at the way Lyons wove Yeats and his poetry into Irish history in the role of actor as well as witness.

VG When you encounter poems by Yeats now, can you distinguish them from your knowledge of the life? Do you think of them as illustrative of their biographical moment, or as distinct objects, complete in themselves?

RF That's a difficult question. The poems do of course exist in a dimension of their own. But certain poems are specially linked to moments in his life, for me; 'Two Songs of a Fool' so clearly reflects the early days of his marriage to George and his worries about Iseult, for instance, and 'Meditations in Time of Civil War' can't be separated from one's idea of him at Ballylee, and patterned against his letters of the time. Other poems mean a lot because I think I know, or infer, a certain agenda or address behind them: I'm sure 'Those Images' is addressed to Dorothy Wellesley, for instance. And 'The Cold Heaven' (a particular favourite of mine) seems to isolate a particular moment of *Sturm und Drang* in his life, and is all the stronger for that. Even before I wrote the biography, I thought the once-fashionable line advanced by Cleanth Brooks and others, that a poet's life was of no importance in considering his or her poems, was pretty questionable. Studying Yeats convinced me that this was wrong.

VG WBY can seem a contradictory and often, to deploy Auden's word, a silly man. On the other hand, he comes across as having been unfailingly loyal and generous towards his friends – a stalwart. Ultimately, would you have been inclined to judge him harshly or sympathetically when you were writing the biography? Has that view changed at all in the intervening years? (Or is this even a useful question? Perhaps you had no personal judgment either way towards him? Perhaps such a judgment might have interfered with your writing of the biography?).

RF You don't have to like someone to write a biography of them, but you do have to feel a certain empathy – even if it has to be what Robert Gerwarth called, when writing about a monster (Reinhard Heydrich) 'cold empathy'. With Yeats it is much easier because there is so much to admire and marvel at: the silliness is there, but so – as you rightly say – is his genius for friendship, his appetite for life, his humour. (All this makes nonsense of the idiotic notion advanced by some obtuse retrospective psychologists that he probably suffered from Asperger's Syndrome). Even the silliness has sympathetic elements in it. One advantage, too, of writing a life on as large a scale as I was allowed to do, is that you build up the person's character as it grows, and certain characteristics (even certain 'tics') develop as their life matures, and become comprehensible and sympathetic.

VG Can you imagine any future biography of WBY by another writer? In what ways do you think that this could differ from yours?

RF This perhaps isn't for me to say. But I think that for someone with as capacious a genius as Yeats, there is always room for new interpretations. Indeed, even while I was writing my biography, other lives of Yeats appeared (one of them, by Terence Brown, very good) and they didn't – I think – make mine redundant. I'm sure, with the publication of the marital correspondence, and the appearance of further volumes of the great edition of *Collected Letters* by John Kelly and others, there will be further biographies. I did, of course, have access to this material in unpublished form for my own researches; but its appearance in print will no doubt galvanize further biographies, from different angles.

VG There are aspects of some later poems that, even after years of reading, I still don't understand. Did you feel when writing the biography that an understanding of the poems would be necessary, or not?

RF Yes, but the understanding isn't always completely rational or analytical, more a sense of intuition. In late poems such as 'The Statues' or 'A Bronze Head', I find a new angle nearly every time I read them, and am still not certain that I've 'got' them completely; 'Among School Children' is another that yields new levels of meaning time and time again. Part of Yeats's genius is to convey a sense of history, destiny, mystical illumination without having to fully 'explain' it. That's true of a poem such as 'The Second Coming', where the mystery is part of the impact, and of the effect. There's also the fact that some of his less successful work can be decoded for insights into his life and mind ('The Grey Rock' for instance, or 'The Gift of Harun Al-Rashid').

VG Knowing him as well as you do, how do you think WBY would have responded to your biography?

RF That's absolutely not for me to say! I was encouraged throughout by the fact that Yeats himself had written, famously, that we need to know about a poet's life. It's one of the epigraphs to my first volume: '[A poet's] life is an experiment in living and those that come after have a right to know it. Above all it is necessary that the lyric poet's life be known that we should understand that his poetry is no rootless flower but the speech of a man.' He also anticipated, as he said more than once to Lady Gregory, that their biographies would be part of Irish history. So he couldn't disapprove of the enterprise. What he'd feel about the execution is something else. When the late Richard Finneran put as the epigraph to his book about editing the *Collected Poems* those lines from 'What Then?', I have to say that I winced. 'Let the fools rage, I swerved in naught / Something to perfection brought'. When his edition wasn't universally well received, it certainly looked like tempting fate.

VG If, through time travel, you'd had the chance to interview WBY, where would you have conducted it – a swish hotel, his home, your office, a café, by correspondence?

RF Probably the wonderfully atmospheric rooms in Woburn Buildings near Euston Station, where he carved out his early life for himself; then later, perhaps, in the Tower, which I find very powerfully atmospheric; I'm very glad that it's to be reopened. Or on Ezra Pound's rooftop terrace in Rapallo, where Yeats spent some winters ... There are so many locations to which he lent his stamp, and where he describes writing. 'Place' was extremely important to him. As to time travel, however, I've never dreamt that I am talking to him, which is the only kind of time travel available to most of us. I used to dream of Parnell when I was writing about him, forty years ago – my first book. A very vivid dream of encountering him in a railway carriage on the way to Rathdrum. Oddly, Yeats has never shown up in my dreams, or not yet.

VG If you could have asked WBY any one question, no matter how trivial or earnest, have you any sense of what that might have been?

RF Impossible question. It wouldn't have been regarding his occult interests, about which he gave so many adept and fudging answers. Nor about what he meant in his book of philosophy, *A Vision*. Perhaps – since the commemorationist fever is upon us – it would be about the Rising and his ambivalence, so subtly and hauntingly expressed in 'Easter 1916', and how and when he decided to endorse it. The trajectory of his opinions during 1916-1922 (a particularly convulsive period in his personal life too) is a subject on which there is, perhaps, more to be said.

VG If you could have him talk through one poem of his with you, which poem might that be?

RF Another impossible question. Perhaps 'Long-Legged Fly', which is so deceptively economical and throws such a wide and enigmatic arc across life, civilizations, the mystery of artistic creation. Also, perhaps, because it is up there with my very favourite Yeats poems. But then I start to think 'No, what about "Sailing To Byzantium"...' And so on.

VG Has anything come to your notice about WBY since writing the biography, that might have materially altered what you wrote?

RF Ronald Schuchard's work on Yeats and music made me think I should have explored his ideas about chanting and rhythm further. Some more material has come to light about his political opinions in the 1930s – but I did get a chance to write a bit more about that, in a subsequent essay. And some official correspondence has just come to light in French archives, which fills out the question of the disinterment at Roquebrune and reburial in Sligo – though it wouldn't materially alter what I wrote in the Epilogue to my second volume. By and large I stand pretty much by what's in those two volumes.

VG From your biography, I get a strong sense of WBY's impressive work ethic, but I'm not sure what he did to relax. Did he ever? Have I missed something?

RF In his youth he went fishing, of course, which is reflected in his poems; I used to amiably argue with the late classical scholar JV Luce as to whether he was likely to have been much good as an angler. He loved swimming in the sea at Rapallo. And though not much of a drinker, and famously careless about what he ate, he liked going out to restaurants and talking with friends: not only in his youth in Bohemian London, but much later. Frederick Ashton, who knew him in the 1920s, described merry evenings in Soho restaurants. Like most people who work very hard, he actually thought of himself as threatened by the besetting sin of idleness – perhaps one of the offshoots of a Protestant upbringing.

VG Were WBY's autobiographical writings more of a help or a hindrance to you?

RF Oh they were wonderful! Not because you could rely on them for factual record – they are deliberately vague, impressionist, uncertain at one level – and carefully disingenuous on another, and much of the content is manipulated to position himself and his friends in a certain niche in Irish history, or to pay off old scores. Comparing early drafts with the finished versions, the excisions and changes are very instructive indeed. But they express so much of his humour, as in *Dramatis Personae*, or summon up the atmosphere of the time, as in *The Trembling of the Veil*, or simply express subtle and quizzical thoughts and self-analysis in such marvellous prose, that they reflect the man in an extraordinarily magnetic way. I do think Yeats's prose writing – like his literary and dramatic criticism – has been neglected, perhaps because the poetry is so rich and all-encompassing. The *Autobiographies* would have to accompany me on a desert island, I think, along with the poems.

VG It was a monumental project. Did your writing of WBY change your subsequent work in any way?

RF I think it taught me to read literary texts more demandingly, especially when manuscript or variant versions are available. And it confirmed my belief that to understand people's lives we need to adhere to chronology rather than themes, while accepting the recurrence of certain patterns: it's in the contingent and unforeseen that the drama lurks. That is where my approach to Yeats's life differed from Richard Ellmann's, revere him though I do; I think it borrowed more from his approach to Joyce. (I still think Ellmann's *James Joyce* is the template of literary biography).

VG Is there anything you're surprised to have never been asked about writing the biography?

RF Many people, including you, have asked if it's difficult for an historian to write about a poet, and I usually point out that you don't have to be a literary critic in order to read poetry. But no-one has ever asked me whether I ever write, or wrote, poetry myself. In fact I did, quite compulsively, between the ages of about fourteen and nineteen. Then it disappeared, like acne. This was fortunate for others as well as myself, but I suspect it did give me some helpful ideas about structure and form: as well as an idea of the yawning gulf between the poetry that is worth reading (and writing), and the stuff that isn't.

VG Is there any other literary figure whose biography you'd be interested in taking on?

RF I think I am going to write a very short book about Seamus Heaney, though it's not a 'Life' in that sense. But these days I'm more interested in group biography, or the way a number of lives intersect and cross-cut at a certain era of history (the subject of my last book, *Vivid Faces,* about the revolutionary generation in Ireland). In any case, it is very hard to think of anyone who would be as inspirational to spend time with, as Yeats – let alone over eighteen years. I'm lucky; I've been spoiled.

Maurice Riordan

EVANESCENT CHARM

WB Yeats, *The Wind Among the Reeds* (Elkin Mathews, London, 1899), cover design by Althea Gyles, Octavo, pp. viii, 108.

I have recently been in correspondence with a physician, a Viennese Jew, who treats those with delusional maladies. As a therapeutic method, he investigates the dreams of his patients with the object of uncovering their symbolical content. I would venture that Dr Freud (for such is my correspondent's name) would be an excellent reader of Mr William Butler Yeats's handsome new volume, *The Wind Among the Reeds*.

It comprises some sixty pages of verses, followed by an almost equal quantity of 'Notes'. In these Mr Yeats recalls the Gaelic lore of his native West of Ireland. In the poet's mind, the personages and fantastical exploits of mythology have combined with his studies in magic. As he observes, 'It is probable that only students of the magical tradition will understand me when I say that "Michael Robartes" is fire reflected in water, and that Hanrahan is fire blown by the wind, and that Aedh, whose name is not merely the Irish form of Hugh, but the Irish for fire, is fire burning by itself.' I am not myself a devotee of Madame Blavatsky and Mr Aleister Crowley, although I would surmise that this approach severely restricts comprehension of the poet's latest volume.

This is in contrast to Mr Yeats's past productions, which sounded (to cite Mr Arnold) the 'Celtic Note' clearly, and can be said to have awakened a sense of natural magic in the imaginative life of simple country folk. Poems such as 'The Stolen Child' and 'The Man Who Dreamed of Faeryland' have the wildness of the Atlantic seaboard and the vigour of untutored speech. They earned the applause of Mr Wilde, among others. In the volume under review, the spirited 'The Fiddler of Dooney' is reminiscent of the former manner – but it is untypical.

During the past decade, the Irish poet has added an interest in French Symbolism to his other spheres. He has had the benefit of Mr Symons's erudition when it comes to the modern Movement among the French Poets. Now we have the *Poésies* of M. Mallarmé to hand (though sadly in the absence of its author), it is apparent that his Celtic symbolism is a dilution of the originating source. The symbolism of the French master is indeed dense, but it is possessed of a potent musical resonance such that it does not warrant exposition. It is happily surrounded by eloquent silence. With this, Mr Yeats cannot compete.

On the contrary, he resorts to the expedient of windy glosses to explain his symbols to his reader. These demand considerable elaboration, as when we are informed that 'I have made the Seven Lights, the constellation of the Bear, lament for the theft of the Rose, and I have made the Dragon, the constellation Draco, the guardian of the Rose, because these constellations move about the pole of the heavens, the ancient Tree of Life in many countries, and are often associated with the Tree of Life in mythology. It is this Tree of Life that I have put into the "Song of Mongan" under its common Irish form of a hazel tree; and, because it had sometimes the stars for fruit, I have hung upon it "the Crooked Plough" and the "Pilot" star, as Gaelic-speaking Irishmen some-times call the Bear and the North star. I have made it an axle-tree in "Aedh hears the Cry of the Sedge", for this was another ancient way of representing it.' Turning to the brief lyric that is last adduced, we find lines of unrequited yearning such as '*Your head will not lie on the breast / Of your beloved in sleep*'; and we are made to infer that the fulfilment of the lover's desire would require the end of the world.

If we set this portion of Mr Yeats's offering aside, and if we also consult his *Poems*, which are reissued along with the new volume, we find ourselves in the presence of a true poet, one whose genius it is to evoke a remote and intangible beauty. I have in mind, from the present gathering, his 'The Song of Wandering Aengus', which disarms us with its unassuming plainness, 'I went out to the hazel wood, / Because a fire was in my head'. The poet then has a vision rather in the manner of those ancient Bards who recounted in the Erse their encounters with a *spéirbhean* or Sky-Woman. Mr Yeats's composition has a more personal inflexion that issues in lines of exquisite lyrical loveliness:

> I will find out where she has gone,
> And kiss her lips and take her hands;
> And walk among long dappled grass,
> And pluck till time and times are done,
> The silver apples of the moon,
> The golden apples of the sun.

In similar vein, the quaintly titled 'Aedh Wishes for the Cloths of Heaven' (I fear the author may have intended the *clothes* of Heaven) paints the night-sky as 'Enwrought with golden and silver light', and concludes:

> But I, being poor, have only my dreams;
> I have spread my dreams under your feet;
> Tread softly because you tread on my dreams.

Such cadences linger in the mind and one is loath to dismiss them from the memory. In rendering so hauntingly what might be described as the heart's cry against necessity, Mr Yeats has no living equal.

I confess that much as I am charmed by such verses, I believe Mr Yeats has now reached the term of his service to the lyric Muse. Elsewhere, we are witnessing the dawn of a new era in the prose school of Messrs Wells, Crane and Conrad, and to some measure in the ballads of Mr Kipling and now of Mr EA Robinson. It may be that Mr Yeats is in step with these advances in his current widely reported efforts to found a national drama in Ireland. As he embarks on the next stage of his endeavours, I recommend to him the Jewish doctor I have mentioned as one who brings scientific rigour to the recording and interpretation of dreams as a remedy for emotional obstructions in the labyrinth of the mind. He might profit from that old adage, 'In dreams begin responsibilities'.

Frank McGuinness

A KICK IN THE HEAD

My first exposure to this artist was as a child attending Buncrana Feis, held that year with disarming modesty in a ballroom called Broadway on our main street, where my cousin Elizabeth O'Haire, along with what seemed like hundreds of her classmates, recited 'The Song Of Wandering Aengus' in a verse speaking competition. All were word perfect, and before saying the poems, contestants gave the author his full, beautiful name, William Butler Yeats, as strange and thrilling a sound as anything in the imagery of the text. If I did not know off by heart each line before, I certainly did by the time the last entrant had finished. Elizabeth did not win, and though I cannot recall the name of the glimmering girl who received first prize, I remember she wore a red dress whose fabric dazzles in my memory, and her face had a spectral beauty – the kind of being I'd learn, later in life, who haunts the man's poetry, so he would, I'm sure, have been very happy to see her scoop 'The silver apples of the moon, / The golden apples of the sun'.

Coming from a tribe of implacable Donegal redheads, we thought our cousin should have walked it. Still, we did not carry this slight to our honour as a lifelong insult, igniting a burning revenge. Insult and revenge – these all too often seemed to typify Yeats and his doings. There were times when despite the overwhelming splendour and the complex lyricism of his intelligence, his poetry intrigued me most for the reckless way he went for his enemies, spitting blood in all directions. Here was a man who could not settle quarrels but insisted on handing out a good hiding to any he believed deserved it. Most wondrously, most impressively, he delivered these acts of assault and battery within the precisely delineated codes and structures of his well-wrought stanzas. That only intensified their elegant brutality. His was a hatred that persisted. What was it for?

It has taken me years to stumble on some explanation for this violence, and here is why I believe he was like himself and no other. Yeats, when it comes down to it, had no or next to no sense of humour. The comedy of his plays – it is a kindness to call it comedy – proves that. Threatening to lacerate whoever provokes him, he takes up the most ridiculous of poses and persists in maintaining them, until even he can see the ludicrous side to his intensity, recording it with a delicacy of form that belies the content. He thereby pulls off one of the greatest ironies in modern poetry, and I love the sheer doggedness of a mind so upstaged and confounded by its own machinations, self-perpetuating, self-defeating. He is then all mouth and no trousers, that most gorgeous and hilarious of combinations.

But put me up against a wall and I'll tell you why I admire him most: for his command of vocabulary, and his power of verbal concision. I have done a fair bit of work now on Greek plays. It is not for his take on Oedipus that I praise Yeats. He misses too often what is most rare and most rough in the playwright Sophocles. No, the poem that obsesses and guides me in all my explorations of that theatre is 'Leda and The Swan'. I know every line, every step of its syntactical choreography, the profound silence following that desolate, bereaved, broken line, 'And Agamemnon dead'. This poem is his greatest play, and within the space of a sonnet Yeats becomes a monumental storyteller as he encompasses the whole Trojan War, its shocks, its sorrows, the cruel mating of god and woman, that strange congress of human with divine, then the casual, cunning, ferocious climax. 'Leda and The Swan' is my key to everything I've tried to write about the Greeks, and it is still 'as cold / And passionate as the dawn' as when I first discovered it.

I admit this with great effort, because for years I fought Yeats. If I grudgingly gave him the time of day, it was not for himself alone, but compared to the puniness of talent in most Irish poets of his day he was at least everything they were not. Such a negative compliment is no basis for saluting the scale of his ambition. As I age, I observe the power he has and always has had on me. I will be troubled for life by certain spells his lines cast, potions stirred by Quattrocentro finger, dining on a mess of shadows that, years before, Rimbaud identified as illuminations, but then turned out to be the opposite. Like the French poet, Yeats had his fair share of darkness. His politics veer from enlightened to the utterly and unforgivably ignorant. Auden in his great elegy to the ghost of Yeats told him, 'You were silly like us'. May we be protected as he was emphatically not protected from much of his silliness, but as I look at the book, *The Collected Poems of William Butler Yeats*, containing the sheer size of his accomplishments, successfully realized, there waiting to be relished on the table beside me, I want so much to make my peace with this most troubling writer. For daring to chance that, he would kick me in the face. Well, he'd try to. He would miss. He's taught me that much.

Joseph O'Neill

POPULATION: I

Since we are familiar with the notion of Yeats as the 'national poet', I thought I'd offer some thoughts on a poem in which the Yeatsian speaker resists the very idea of Irish nationality – 'The Lake Isle of Innisfree'. It's a perfectly verbalized escapist fantasy in which, you might say, Robinson maroons himself on Walden's island. But what kind of escape is this? From the opening insurrectionary declaration – 'I will arise', the prefix 'a' intensifying the already potent 'rise' – we're on notice that the poem is concerned, first and foremost, with the question of political action.

The poem's action is simple enough: an either supine or prone speaker announces that he (or, why not, she) will forthwith get up and go, from a grey place of roadways and pavements, to a small uninhabited island in a lake, and establish himself there in solitude, simple self-sufficiency and peace. The topographic specificity is important. The described retreat isn't a mainland woods like Thoreau's, or a desert wasteland of the kind we associate with St Anthony the Great, or, if we venture into the world of Howard Hughes, a Las Vegas hotel penthouse. Our would-be solitary is contemplating isolation in the strict sense – aloneness on an island.

What kind of islander will he make? If he were a hermit, his religious vocation would place him and his prayers at the service of mankind. But this off-grid settler has no such agenda and indeed seems intent on breaking the connection to his fellow man. He will provide only for himself. His plan is to build a 'small' (i.e., studio) cabin and to plant no more than nine rows of beans; and, with the sounds and sights of nature as his medium, he will commune only with himself. He will be an extremist not only of self-rule but also, in his repudiation of all human doings beyond the watery margin of his new territory, an extremist of self-identification. That is, he will see himself as purely self-identical; in others, to the extent that he will see them at all, he will see nothing but otherness. In political terms, and turning PH Pearse's dictum on its head, he will reject the identifying agglomeration of individuals that makes nationhood possible.

In this context, it is significant that the dream territory is a miniscule version of the national territory. On its tiny scale, what differentiates Innisfree from everywhere else is precisely the differentiating geophysical characteristic that underlies the Irish claim to nationality and statehood: insularity. Innisfree is therefore an enclave, an imagined island nation-state within another imagined island nation-state, Ireland – for this is 1888. Which makes one ask: isn't the isle actually a colony within a colony? What is a settler-cultivator of newly seized land if not a colonist? And so 'The Lake Isle' is an Irishman's anxious reaction to the decolonizing meaning of 'Irish'. A word that previously designated one's provenance and social brand and sentimental attachments has suddenly become an irresistible determiner that rolls one, whether consenting or protesting, into a perilous, unstable, necessarily coercive political mass. Nationality, in the sense of a rough and random and consequential identity one cannot escape, has arrived. What a relief, then, to dream of a one-man nation, and to dream, while one's at it, of a man-state of one's own, a state of oneness, a state in which a man is an island, a state that serves as a neo-colonial refuge from the nationalism that now presses on one and on one's old way of sensing oneself to be Irish, a state in which one lives with oneself alone, among extranational bees and crickets and linnets.

I will arise and go now, and go to Innisfree ... The declaration is repeated in the final stanza. The speaker's situation has not changed. Our fantastical insurgent is still where he started, lying either on his back or on his face, and he's not going anywhere. A new Irishness rises about him like a flood, and must claim him.

Medbh McGuckian

KNIGHTS OF FAITH AND RESIGNATION

WB Yeats, *In The Seven Woods* (Dun Emer Press, 1903).

TS Eliot in 1940, after Yeats's death, praised him as 'one of those few whose history is the history of their own time', his ability being, 'after becoming unquestionably the master, to remain always a contemporary'. The sonnets in this collection are perfect specimens of courtly love worthy of Sidney, Shakespeare, Blake: they can be read a thousand times without their mastery being eclipsed. The more political and prophetic poems with their choral refrains are less memorable, as Frank O'Connor wrote in *The Irish Statesman*, 1925:

> Now, what do I find wrong with Yeats? I find this; that never, at any time
> or for any occasion whatsoever, does his art come into touch with life,
> with the world around us. His poems have no real trouble of spirit
> behind them, in a word, they are complacent. I do object to the
> assumption that this verse represents Irish literature.

O'Connor's qualms are echoed by another contemporary reviewer of the collection, CK Chesterton, who wrote:

> Mr WB Yeats, in his exquisite and piercing elfin poetry, describes the
> elves as lawless; they plunge in innocent anarchy on the unbridled
> horses of the air [...] It is a dreadful thing to say that Mr WB Yeats does
> not understand fairy land. But I do say it. He is an ironical Irishman, full
> of intellectual reactions. He is not stupid enough to understand
> fairyland. [...] Mr Yeats read into elfland all the righteous insurrection of
> his own race.

Be all that as it may, he had the perception to place in the exact middle of the collection his first breakthrough modernist poem, 'Adam's Curse', which, while it assumes that only men can write poetry, aligns it with the feminine tasks of sewing and household chores. The theme is from Castiglione's *The Book of the Courtier*, on grace and style: 'To avoid affectation in every way possible [...] to practice in all things a certain *sprezzatura* [nonchalance], so as to conceal all art and make whatever is done or said appear to be without effort and almost without any thought about it'.

I have heard these poems recited lovingly by heart, seen them quoted on postcards, and eternally remembered as instinctive, spontaneous utterance of feeling when the drafts show endless rewriting. And when we were young ourselves there was no folly in our being comforted by them.

Queen's University, Belfast boasts a first edition of the 1903 *In the Seven Woods* in its Special Collection. You can hold and read but not borrow it. The inscription is erased but it is clearly unsigned. It is hand-printed by Yeats's sister, Lolly, of the Cuala Press, on locally produced Irish linen paper of a vellum-like texture. David Holderman, in his study of it, 'Much Labouring', singles it out for praise as Yeats's first modernist book, noting that critics often dismiss it as a transitional effort, less accomplished and interesting than the well-known works of his earlier and later periods. It was conceived and collated during the Year of the Big Wind, in the benumbed aftermath of Maud Gonne's marriage, in the Dublin around the time in which *Ulysses* is set. He wrote in one copy: 'This is the first book of mine that is a pleasure to look at – a pleasure whether open or shut.'

It was intentionally an art object with its exclusive typeface in 14 point Caslon old style font, its tightly unified two-page layouts closing the gaps between the poems, its hand sewn creamy paper. Its simplicity was aimed at an aristocratic or middle-class elite whilst reflecting the egalitarian ideals of William Morris's Kelmscott Press. Red ink was used periodically, no bleaching materials, the spine was unlabelled in a print run of 325 for the price of 10s 6d, which was two months' wages for the workgirls at the Saggart Mill. It was presold to many subscribers and book collectors who resold it in America for one to five pounds.

It received limited public notice at the time since Yeats refused to send it to the Dublin papers that had previously attacked him. Joyce referred to it as 'five lines of text and ten pages of notes about the folk and fishgods of Dundrum, printed by the weird sisters'. Other comments include: 'What the effect on the Irish mind will be of such attempts to make live again the ideals of long ago, no one can say; but we are sure that Mr. Yeats and his sister in this thin white volume are serving their country in "the old high way of love".' And: He 'elects to chew the cud of sweet and bitter Irish fancies with his feet in an Irish bog and his head in a rainbow'. One Chicago review cited its overall 'combination of warm democratic sympathy and high breeding', which summarizes the contradictory tensions played out in Yeats's conflicting loyalties to both antiquity (as cherished by Lady Gregory), and the contemporary violence (as advocated by Maud Gonne MacBride).

The period of its composition was for Yeats one of near dormancy: his energies were distracted by mystical pursuits, essays and prose fiction, the revision of previous volumes, political and dramatic involvement (especially with the Abbey Theatre), not to speak of physical / erotic affairs with women in London. Despite Frank O'Connor's claim, this is the first of his books whose title is taken from the actual experienced world, albeit the charmed and magical financially secure home of eighteenth-century or medieval patronage he had found and succumbed to in Coole Park. A large number of the many drafts of the included poems are meticulously typed and corrected by pen on Lady Gregory's blue stationery. He pays due tribute to his specific inspiration, the extensive forested estate which funded and fostered his development, like a modern day Arts Council grant or University residency, or research travel award.

In the first edition he included two plays which were later replaced by three poems. There are then fourteen poems or half a book, the size of a pamphlet. They are not in the order of writing; 'Red Hanrahan' was the first to be written, in 1893, but is positioned eighth, for example. The opening poem is the first of three sonnets, not fully rhymed, paying homage to the elite but natural retreat from the city that earlier poems had yearned for. Seven seems to be here a mystically satisfying number and the collection seems to lean into a sense of achieved contentment, if not happiness. The two main women in his life are not on stage here but obliquely personified as 'Quiet' and 'bitterness'. The latter has been 'forgot awhile' in the classical platonic Urbino of Augustan patronage, but no sooner has he acknowledged his withdrawal than the second poem flies instinctively back to the young Muse whose 'apple blossom bosom' transcends the faint eroticism of the lime flowers.

Kierkegaard in *Fear and Trembling* avoids the traditional romantic hero by conjuring an anti-hero, a good man, simple yet noble, the knight of faith rather than the knight of infinite resignation, whose central ordeal of losing and gaining a loved one is close to that experienced and celebrated – even if there are few consolations – by Yeats's poetic persona. The stock fairytale is absurd, the movement back to the finite after the movement of infinity that the poet cannot make. As a good man he is able to abide by the temporal after having surrendered it.

> A youth falls in love with a princess and the whole of his life is bound up with this love, although the relation is such that it is impossible for it to realize itself or to translate itself from ideality into reality. The slaves of the finite and those frogs who inhabit the swamps of life will naturally cry out: 'What a stupid love-story! The rich brewer's widow would make just as good a match.' ... The knight of infinite resignation does not follow their advice; he refuses to surrender his love even for all the glory in the world ... He is not a coward; he is not afraid to let love steal into his remote and secret thoughts; he is not afraid to let it wind itself in innumerable coils round every ligament of his consciousness ... He

experiences a voluptuous pleasure in allowing love to run shuddering through his nerves ...When he has wholly absorbed this love and plunged deeply into it, he does not lack the courage to attempt everything and to risk all ... He has the strength to be able to concentrate the whole content of his life and the whole significance of reality into a single desire which has utterly changed him.

The difficulty of living as the knight of faith is that temporality takes time, love is no longer self-sustaining and frozen eternally, the blissful seizing of the finite has its dark side:

Thus to obtain the princess is a marvellous thing ... to live with her in gladness and in joy day after day ... to see at every moment the sword hanging over the head of the beloved, and finding no peace in the suffering of resignation, but instead joy by virtue of the absurd – how wonderful that is.

WB Yeats

EASTER 1916

I have met them at close of day
Coming with vivid faces
From counter or desk among grey
Eighteenth-century houses.
I have passed with a nod of the head
Or polite meaningless words,
Or have lingered awhile and said
Polite meaningless words,
And thought before I had done
Of a mocking tale or a gibe
To please a companion
Around the fire at the club,
Being certain that they and I
But lived where motley is worn:
All changed, changed utterly:
A terrible beauty is born.

That woman's days were spent
In ignorant good-will,
Her nights in argument
Until her voice grew shrill.
What voice more sweet than hers
When, young and beautiful,
She rode to harriers?
This man had kept a school
And rode our winged horse;
This other his helper and friend
Was coming into his force;
He might have won fame in the end,
So sensitive his nature seemed,
So daring and sweet his thought.
This other man I had dreamed
A drunken, vainglorious lout.
He had done most bitter wrong
To some who are near my heart,
Yet I number him in the song;
He, too, has resigned his part
In the casual comedy;
He, too, has been changed in his turn,
Transformed utterly:
A terrible beauty is born.

Hearts with one purpose alone
Through summer and winter seem
Enchanted to a stone
To trouble the living stream.
The horse that comes from the road,
The rider, the birds that range
From cloud to tumbling cloud,
Minute by minute they change;
A shadow of cloud on the stream
Changes minute by minute;
A horse-hoof slides on the brim,
And a horse plashes within it;
The long-legged moor-hens dive,
And hens to moor-cocks call;
Minute by minute they live:
The stone's in the midst of all.

Too long a sacrifice
Can make a stone of the heart.
O when may it suffice?
That is Heaven's part, our part
To murmur name upon name,
As a mother names her child
When sleep at last has come
On limbs that had run wild.
What is it but nightfall?
No, no, not night but death;
Was it needless death after all?
For England may keep faith
For all that is done and said.
We know their dream; enough
To know they dreamed and are dead;
And what if excess of love
Bewildered them till they died?
I write it out in a verse –
MacDonagh and MacBride
And Connolly and Pearse
Now and in time to be,
Wherever green is worn,
Are changed, changed utterly:
A terrible beauty is born.

Anne Michaels

AT CLOSE OF DAY

I have met them at close of day
neither named nor unknown,
not force of will
nor desire. Perhaps
prayer. Not capsized
nor at sea. Not still, perhaps
held.

You said,
at the end, you wanted
to keep your eyes open,
to miss nothing.

I miss you. Not entreaty
nor regret. Not future
nor past: these always last.
Of course, touch and warm
weight. Of course
breath and again. Of course
what word can be heard.

Not loss
nor absence. Perhaps
soul. Not inside
nor outside: dusk's
doorway. Not
alone.

WB Yeats

THE LOVER'S SONG

Bird sighs for the air,
Thought for I know not where,
For the womb the seed sighs.
Now sinks the same rest
On mind, on nest,
On straining thighs.

John Glenday

BIRD SIGHS FOR THE AIR
sunt lacrimae rerum

Bird sighs for the air? There are those
who would insist air sighs for the bird.
All that bluster and expanse nothing more

than a reaching out towards the least
fraction of itself – a flicker of wren through
summer briar, one note from a firecrest's song.

Everything is the shape of the longing
it was built to hold. Even the olive wears
the curve of the stone it carries in its heart.

And you? Your empty arms confess
to everything they held once and then lost,
or longed to hold but never came to hold.

Your arms, filled, all those things
you are holding now – things you desire,
things you have yet to lose.

HOW YEATS ARE YOU?
– Questions set by **Spare Ribh**

Score

1. Just how crazy was Jane?
   A. Not as daft as Tom the Lunatic   1
   B. Mad as the mist and snow   2
   C. Crazier than that King Goll, who was clearly just trying it on   3

2. What was Yeats's favourite rhyme for 'love'?
   A. Above   3
   B. Enough   2
   C. Brazilian mango grove   1

3. On what did Yeats most like to write?
   A. Upon the window pane   2
   B. Upon a house shaken by the land agitation   1
   C. Upon a dying lady   3

4. Which was Yeats's favourite rose?
   A. The rose upon the rood of time   1
   B. The far-off, most secret, and inviolate rose   2
   C. Nine-bean Rose   3

5. What should Michael Robartes have done about his double vision?
   A. Gone on a blind date with Crazy Jane   3
   B. Gone back to 1893, to help out with 'The Two Trees'   2
   C. Gone to Specsavers   1

6. What did Yeats usually wish for, blowing out his birthday candles?
   A. A theme   3
   B. The cloths of heaven   2
   C. That his beloved would croak   1

7. Where did Yeats go to relax?
   A. Among school children   3
   B. Galway races   3
   C. The Municipal Gallery, again   3

8. Was Yeats fond of rhetorical questions?   0

9. What was Yeats's favourite holiday destination?
   A. Wherever the Statesman was going (usually Avalon)   1
   B. Byzantium   2
   C. Coole Park (the all-inclusive package was a steal)   3

10. Which male acappella group sang at Yeats's burial in Drumcliffe churchyard?

    A. The Three Hermits   1

    B. The Seven Sages   1

    C. Sixteen Dead Men   1

11. First publication of which Yeats poem was sponsored by Maguire and Paterson Match Co?

    A. 'No Second Troy'   1

    B. 'A Stick of Incense'   2

    C. 'In Memory of Eva Goore-Booth and Con Markiewicz'   3

12. The Fiddler of Dooney was:

    A. A Co Sligo tax accountant   3

    B. The inspiration for the musical, *Fiddler on the Roof*   2

    C. Yehudi Menuhin   0

13. The 'long-legged bird' of 'Lapis Lazuli' is:

    A. His long-legged fly, on stilts   1

    B. The Guinness Toucan   2

    C. Maud Gonne   3

14. What happened the circus animals after their desertion?

    A. Crazy Jane caught and ate them (with a side of salad, don't you know)   2

    B. They're allegedly buried in Drumcliffe   3

    C. Last seen performing with Duffy's (though a little worse for wear)   0

15. Yeats's favourite reality TV show would be:

    A. *The Undateables*   3

    B. *Embarrassing Bodies*   3

    C. *The Voice*   3

Add up your points. Find out how Yeats you are.

Answers on page 200

Olivia O'Leary

YEATS: PART OF THE LITURGY

She was my radio producer and she was giving me her email address:
Sile.Yeats@rte.ie 'Yeats as in the poet?' I checked. 'Well, yeah!' she said,
and then it suddenly struck me. 'Are you related?' She burst out laughing:
'Ah come on! With this physiog, how could I escape him?' Of course.
The faun-like face, the shock of dark hair falling over her forehead. I had
been working for years with the poet's granddaughter. How could I not
have noticed?

Síle was a proper journalist, trained in the hard old school of the *Irish
Press*. When she died all too young at the age of fifty-two, we missed her
generosity and her professionalism. Síle was one of us.

WB Yeats was one of us. He might have hated that, particularly with
the Nietzschean contempt for the common people he developed in later
life. He was one of us because we claimed him. He helped create the
necessary myth which built a nation, and he knew it. He supplied the
magic: the work suffused with folklore, fairies, heroes and heroines. To
an Irish Catholic child like me, the mystery and symbolism of Yeats's
poetry was served up on the same plate as transubstantiation and the
immaculate conception. 'It's a mystery,' we reassured one another,
'You're not supposedta understand it'. So we chanted 'The Stolen Child'
and 'The song of Wandering Aengus' in the same way as we sang
'Tantum Ergo' and sniffed the incense at Benediction. We didn't
understand a word of it but we knew it was lovely.

We were used to priests, and everything we knew about Yeats made
him sound like a priest. He dressed in the special vestments of his
profession and lived in a sort of druid's tower. He took himself very
seriously and lectured everybody else about what they should do. And he
worshipped at the altar of nationalism. He might have had some doubts
about that, but we had none. I have sat in the press gallery in Dáil
Éireann and heard generations of Irish politicians quoting 'Easter 1916'.
People who wouldn't know a terrible beauty from a pint of Guinness
will quote those famous lines of Yeats with a quiver in their voices.
Whether he had meant to or not, he immortalised and validated the
leaders of the Rising almost as much as did the 1918 Sinn Féin election
victory. What chance did John Redmond's ghost have against lines like
that?

Indeed, when Northern Ireland erupted in the late 1960s, 'Easter 1916'
came to be regarded by some politicians as dangerous. When Conor
Cruise O'Brien warned in the Dáil in October 1971 that we were drifting

towards civil war because we had thoughtlessly paid lip service to the territorial claim over Northern Ireland, he quoted the poem selectively: 'It seemed as if we lived, as Yeats once said, where motley was worn and we did not have to mean what we said.'

At this, Charles Haughey, brooding in silent disgrace on the government backbenches since the arms trial eighteen months earlier, roared: 'Finish the quotation.' O'Brien refused. 'Finish the quotation,' demanded Haughey, going on to say: 'I do not like to hear the words of Yeats prostituted.' What Haughey wanted to hear were the words:

> All changed, changed utterly:
> A terrible beauty is born.

O'Brien explained to the Dáil a year later why he refused to speak those words: 'What is the relevance of that terrible beauty to the events of our own time? Where is this terrible beauty being born? What can that be but a reverence (*sic*) in a romantic and exalted sense to the IRA campaign?'

Irish politicians quote Yeats more than any other writer because he was, after all, one of them. For six years, he was a member of the Seanad and they quote his speeches almost as often as his poems. And Yeats was your only man for the big occasions. On the day the IRA ceasefire was announced on 31 August 1994, An Taoiseach Albert Reynolds quoted from 'Remorse for Intemperate Speech':

> Out of Ireland have we come.
> Great hatred, little room,
> Maimed us at the start.

At the time of the 2010 EU/IMF bail-out, opposition finance spokesman Michael Noonan lambasted the government for selling out the sovereignty of the Irish people. Inevitably, he 'quoted 'September 1913':

> Was it for this the wild geese spread
> The grey wing upon every tide ...

Noonan, by now Finance Minister, turned to Yeats's 'Easter 1916' when marking Ireland's emergence from the bailout in October 2014 with a kinder budget, explaining:

> Too long a sacrifice
> Can make a stone of the heart.

Yeats could be put to everyday use as well. The Mayo deputy, Michael Ring, quoted from 'Sailing to Byzantium' when criticising government withdrawal of medical cards for the elderly. Yes, you've guessed it: 'That is no country for old men'.

Irish people aren't shy about quoting Yeats because we all learned him at school. Everybody knows him so you're not really showing off. To ask Irish people whether they like Yeats is pointless. It's like asking English people whether they like Shakespeare. Yeats just is. He's part of the liturgy.

English friends will often tell me that they like the later poems, not the earlier 'airy-fairy stuff', as they see it. But the richness of Yeats is the full span of his life and his work. You can grow old with Yeats, be comfortable with poems like 'Adam's Curse' and yet look back with such pleasure on the early music.

I remember a real sense of having come full circle when my ten year old daughter arrived home from school, full of 'The Song of Wandering Aengus'. We tossed lines at one another, and she was triumphant when she could remember one I had forgotten. Together we skipped along the hollow and hilly lands of the last verse and then stood silent in the sunny kitchen, delighted with ourselves.

That's part of being Irish. That's magic. That's Yeats.

Bill Whelan

MUSIC FOR WORDS PERHAPS

It was the late spring of 1989 and Noel Pearson, Artistic Director and Chairman of the Board of the National Theatre, peered at me over his desk in Abbey Street. 'How well do you know your Yeats plays?' he enquired. He had asked me to come in and discuss a potential theatre project. Apparently, the noted American theatre director, author and scholar, James Flannery, would be coming to the Abbey to direct an annual WB Yeats Theatre Festival. Coca-Cola, whose CEO Don Keough was a big Yeats admirer, would be funding this. I had to confess that apart from seeing productions of *At the Hawk's Well* and *The Death of Cuchulain* in my twenties, I was ignorant of the dramatic works of the founder of our National Theatre. 'Well, you'd better read up on them so,' Noel advised, while reaching for the phone and asking the voice on the other end to bring up a copy of the collected plays for me right away. 'What!?' he blinked, 'We don't have any? Well, send somebody out to Eason's will you, and buy a few copies. We're going to be needing them.'

I headed home with a book of plays and a bag of ironies; the irony that a copy of Yeats's plays was not readily available in the theatre he founded; the irony that it was going to take an Irish-American to ignite some action within the theatre to produce his plays. And of course, Coca-Cola was hardly a company whose brand might evoke images of Cathleen the daughter of Houlihan or of Cuchulain bleeding on a pillar-stone.

There was something else nagging at me as the time for rehearsals drew near. Understandably I was anxious and somewhat in awe, not only because of Yeats's legendary position in Irish letters, but also because the poet himself seemed to have had very strong views on the role of music as an accompaniment to his verse. The recordings of Yeats reading his own work, his various pronouncements on the style of music he wanted and his admiration for the psaltery of Florence Farr, all pointed to his taste for the most minimal of tonal involvement with his verse. This is hardly surprising though, given his reputation for being profoundly tone-deaf and his inability to distinguish one tune from another. I had heard that he only recognized the National Anthem when people stood up around him.

And so, the prospect of finding myself in some kind of musical mine-field was much to the fore of my thinking when James Flannery arrived in Dublin in that summer of 1989 to begin the work of producing and directing the first season of the festival. His passionate conviction was that Yeats was not simply a poet in the theatre, but a poet of the theatre.

W.B. YEATS – OCCULTIST!

WORDS - KEVIN JACKSON · PICTURES - HUNT EMERSON

W.B. YEATS! GREATEST IRISH POET EVAH!

NOBEL PRIZE WINNER!

SENATOR AND NATIONAL HERO!

BUT ALSO PASSIONATE OCCULTIST!

BORN IN 1865, YEATS SPENT HIS CHILDHOOD WITH TALES OF THE SUPERNATURAL! HIS FAMILY AND NEIGHBOURS TOLD HIM OF GHOSTS... FAIRIES... AND THE BANSHEE!

AS A TEENAGER HE BECAME OBSESSED WITH THE MYSTICAL CULT OF **THEOSOPHY** AND THE WISDOM OF THE EAST...

IN JANUARY 1888, HE ATTENDED A SÉANCE! THE SPIRIT HE SUMMONED HURLED HIM AGAINST THE WALL!

AND EVERYONE WENT INTO CONVULSIONS!

IT WAS YEARS BEFORE HE DARED TO ATTEND ANOTHER SÉANCE!

HE MOVED TO LONDON AND PUBLISHED A BOOK ABOUT IRISH FOLKLORE. HE SOON BECAME KNOWN AS THE MAN WHO SPOKE WITH FAIRIES...

MR. YEATS INTRODUCES MR. GEORGE MOORE TO THE QUEEN OF THE FAIRIES

AFTER MAX BEERBOHM

HE DABBLED IN STRANGE ARTS... ALCHEMY...ASTROLOGY...MESMERISM...

HE BEGAN TO POSE AS A MAGUS... HIS NEXT-DOOR NEIGHBOUR WAS CONVINCED HE WAS CASTING SPELLS ON HER HUSBAND, AND WENT WHITE WITH TERROR WHEN SHE SAW HIM!

BUT HIS CAREER AS A MAGICIAN REALLY TOOK OFF WHEN HE JOINED THE ORDER OF THE GOLDEN DAWN ... AND MET...

C'EST MOI AGAIN!

666

ALEISTER CROWLEY!

THEY GOT OFF TO A BAD START WHEN YEATS WAS UNIMPRESSED BY THE BEAST'S POETRY...

SHITE AND ONIONS! YOU CALL THIS STUFF POETRY!

CROWLEY WAS ANGRY BUT NOT INTIMIDATED! HE DESCRIBED YEATS' RESPONSE AS...

BILIOUS JEALOUSY!!

FOR THE REST OF HIS DAYS, CROWLEY WOULD DISMISS THE IRISH POET AS

A LANK, DISHEVELLED DEMONOLOGIST...

MEANWHILE, YEATS CONTINUED HIS OCCULT MALARKY OUTSIDE THE GOLDEN DAWN.

HE TOOK HIS FRIEND GEORGE RUSSELL TO A GENTEEL TEA PARTY... RUSSELL WAS TERRIFIED! THE PARLOUR WAS "INFESTED WITH YELLOW DEVILS!"

ON A VISIT TO GALWAY, YEATS DID A "LUNAR EVOCATION" AND SUMMONED THREE MANIFESTATIONS — THE GODDESS DIANA...

...A CENTAUR...

... AND THE THIRD - A SORT OF MIX OF THE TWO!

TO BOOST HIS VISIONARY POWERS, WBY BEGAN TO TAKE MIND-ALTERING DRUGS... IN PARIS HE LEARNED TO SMOKE HASHISH...

HEY— DON'T BOGART THAT JOINT, WILLY...

...AND IN LONDON HE TRIED MESCALINE, BUT GAVE IT UP AS IT GAVE HIM BREATHING PROBLEMS!

HE ALSO COLLABORATED WITH AN ALCHEMIST FRIEND WHO THOUGHT HE COULD MANUFACTURE AN ELIXIR OF LIFE, WHICH HE TESTED ON RABBITS...

I'M A VERY VERY OLD BUNNY..

BUT THE MOST IMPORTANT OUTCOME OF ALL THIS OCCULT ACTIVITY WAS THE RAISING OF A SPIRIT AT A SÉANCE...

IT WAS LEO AFRICANUS- A 16TH CENTURY SPANISH-ARAB EXPLORER... WHO, AT THIS SÉANCE, SPOKE WITH A DISTINCT IRISH BROGUE!

LEO VISITED YEATS AGAIN AND AGAIN OVER THE YEARS! THEY BECAME GREAT CHUMS...

YOU'RE MY BEST FRIEND...

SO YE ARE!

HELLO DERE! WOULD YEZ HAVE A MISTER YEATS AMONGST YEZ?

...OR SOMETIMES LIKE MASTER AND STUDENT...

YEATS BEGAN TO WRITE NEW TYPES OF POEM IN WHICH HE WOULD THRASH OUT THE OLD PHILOSOPHICAL BLETHER BETWEEN TWO SPEAKERS — ONE BASED ON HIMSELF, THE OTHER ON AFRICANUS...

'TIS!

'TISN'T!

MEANWHILE, THE ORDER OF THE GOLDEN DAWN FELL INTO CIVIL WAR! CROWLEY WAS SENT OFF TO THE TEMPLE IN HAMMERSMITH TO NICK MAGICAL EQUIPMENT...

SWAG

HE WAS SEEN OFF BY THE POLICE...

BUT HE CAME BACK TWO DAYS LATER IN FULL HIGHLAND REGALIA AND A "MASK OF OSIRIS"...

HOOTS!

THIS TIME, HE WAS SEEN OFF BY ONE OF YEATS' OCCULTIST FRIENDS, EDWARD HUNTER — A KEEN BOXER!

BIFF!

OW! YOU HAVEN'T HEARD THE LAST OF ME, YOU SHABBY IRISH FRAUD!

WITH CROWLEY OUT OF THE PICTURE, YEATS BEGAN TO CHECK OUT OTHER ASPECTS OF THE SUPERNATURAL!

HE LOVED BRAM STOKER'S DRACULA!

HE EVEN PLANNED A TRIP TO TRANSYLVANIA, THOUGH THIS NEVER CAME OFF...

A SHAME... I COULD MURDER A NICE TASTY POET...

AND HE BECAME CONVINCED THAT IT WAS POSSIBLE TO TRAVEL IN TIME! FOR YEARS HE WAS A FAN OF A BOOK ENTITLED AN ADVENTURE (1911), WHICH TOLD OF TWO OXFORD DONS WHO FIND THEMSELVES IN VERSAILLES AT THE TIME OF LOUIS XV...

IN 1909, WB YEATS WAS MIXED UP IN YET ANOTHER OCCULT RUCK WITH CROWLEY!

...WHO WAS THREATENING TO PUBLISH THE SECRETS OF THE GOLDEN DAWN!

YEATS TRIED TO FEND OFF THIS OUTRAGE BY A TRICK OF COPYRIGHT— HE HAD THE RITUALS PUBLISHED IN LATIN!

ipset lorem quaecunx

HANG ON A MO... WAS THAT A "SIC" OR A "HOC"?

IT FAILED! CROWLEY PUBLISHED, AND THEN WON THE APPEAL BROUGHT BY THE GOLDEN DAWN...

THZZP!

MEANWHILE, YEATS WAS RETURNING TO HIS OLD PASSION FOR SPIRITUALISM!

A LOT OF HIS POETRY AT THE TIME WAS WRITTEN AS A KIND OF 'COLLABORATION' WITH HIS SPIRIT GUIDE...

"THERE WAS A YOUNG LASS OF KILKENNY..."

"WHO'D SELL YOU HER SOUL FOR A PENNY!"

YEATS WAS CALLED IN TO HELP WHEN A FRIEND'S SÉANCE PRODUCED A FLOOD OF ABUSIVE SPIRIT WRITING...

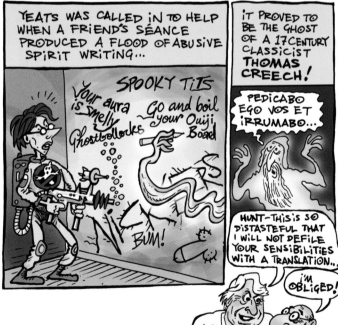

SPOOKY TITS

Your aura is smelly

Go and boil your Ouiji Board

Ghostbollocks

BUM!

IT PROVED TO BE THE GHOST OF A 17 CENTURY CLASSICIST THOMAS CREECH!

PEDICABO EGO VOS ET IRRUMABO...

HUNT—THIS IS SO DISTASTEFUL THAT I WILL NOT DEFILE YOUR SENSIBILITIES WITH A TRANSLATION...

I'M OBLIGED!

BUT YEATS WAS **MOST** DISMAYED WHEN ANOTHER FRIEND TOLD HIM THAT, WHEN **POUND** ENTERED THE ROOM HE HAD **SEVEN PHANTOM BLACK DOGS** WITH HIM, "BARKING AND CIRCLING ROUND HIM"... WBY WAS CONSUMED WITH JEALOUSY!

THE SECOND HALF OF W.B. YEATS' LIFE WAS EVEN MORE EVENTFUL THAN THE FIRST! HE MARRIED A **MUCH YOUNGER WOMAN** WHO PROVED TO BE A BRILLIANT MEDIUM!

Domestic Bliss
in the Yeats' household

HE HAD AN OPERATION TO RESTORE HIS SEXUAL POTENCY...

HE MOVED INTO AN ANCIENT TOWER, WHERE HE COMMUNED WITH IRISH SPIRITS FROM THE 18TH CENTURY...

SLÁINTE!

AND YOURSELF!

HE RETURNED TO HIS EARLY INTEREST IN INDIAN MYSTICISM...

IN DREAMS AND VISIONS HE TIME-TRAVELLED BACK TO ANCIENT BYZANTIUM...

FEK!

IN POEMS, HE SAW HIMSELF AS A METALLIC TOY BIRD — A PLAYTHING FOR "LORDS AND LADIES OF BYZANTIUM"...

USING HIS WIFE'S SPIRIT MESSAGES, HE WROTE A HUGE AND STRANGE BOOK CALLED "A VISION", WHICH EXPLAINS HIS THEORIES OF HISTORICAL CYCLES...

I HAVE A THEORY!

THAT'S NOT WHAT I MEANT!

KJ

HE

MUCH OF YEATS' LATER POETRY WAS BASED ON THEORIES OUTLINED IN "A VISION". POSSIBLY HIS GREATEST POEM FROM THIS TIME WAS A TERRIFYING VISION OF THE GREAT BEAST THAT WOULD DOMINATE A NEW AGE OF SAVAGERY! IT'S CALLED "THE SECOND COMING"...

"AND WHAT ROUGH BEAST, ITS HOUR COME ROUND AT LAST, SLOUCHES TOWARDS BETHLEHEM TO BE BORN?"

'WB Yeats – Occultist!' was first published over five issues
of *Fortean Times*, numbers 309 – 313 (2013/2014).

Hunt Emerson has drawn cartoons and comic strips since the early
1970s. His work has appeared in publications as diverse as *The Beano*,
Fiesta, *Melody Maker*, and *The Wall Street Journal*.
He has published around thirty comic books and albums,
including *The Rime of the Ancient Mariner*, *Lady Chatterley's Lover*,
Casanova's Last Stand, and Dante's *Inferno*.
'WB Yeats – Occultist!' is one of an ongoing series of
Great Occultists he and Kevin Jackson produce for *Fortean Times*.
He lives in Birmingham.
His website is **largecow.com**

Kevin Jackson is a writer, filmmaker, critic, and broadcaster.
He is a luminary of the College of Pataphysics,
a student of vampirism, and his totem animal is the Moose.

THE WILD SWANS OF COOLE. By William
Butler Yeats. 114 pages. Macmillan.

The world loves to weigh its hypothetical losses—
particularly in the domain of art, where the deflection of a craftsman who has made a noteworthy contribution in one field and has subsequently directed
his talents into other channels becomes a theme of
exhaustless speculation. To say what a poet or a
dramatist might have done, if he had not done something else, is a species of criticism in which the haz-
ards of refutation are slight, a circumstance which
possibly accounts for its wide dissemination. To
estimate achievements which—in the nature of
things—cannot exist is a facile form of appre-
ciation, a mode of appraisal perhaps too patronizing
to be prized. William Butler Yeats has come in
for occasional doses of this sedative in the shape of
recurrent sighs over the loss which his absorption in
the Irish Literary Theatre movement involved to
his lyric output. One recalls Mr. Weygandt, in
Irish Plays and Playwrights, raising the question
whether the world shall win " adequate compensa-
tion" for the "lost lyrics" of the Yeats of the nineties.
Other voices, raised in a similar query, emphasize
their point by pouncing upon the lyric passages in
Yeats' dramatic poetry as though these were hares of
the chase—triumphant trophies of vindication. The
defect of all such puzzling is, of course, a failure to
take account of, or at any rate to credit, the inner
creative impulses of the artist, which are pretty
generally at the root of the deflection and pretty
generally unanswerable. The appearance of a new
volume of Yeats' verse, The Wild Swans of Coole,
may serve to fan the embers of speculation. There
are not, however, among these forty poems any

which are destined to strengthen the contention of the mourners over the "lost lyrics." Despite flashes of the old magic, and passages which glow with Yeats' haunting fervor, there is an absence of that sustained mystic charm which pervaded the earlier collections. Nor is the folk flavor so delicately mirrored as it used to be. Indeed, the mood of the collection is largely retrospective—a fact of which the poet seems recurrently conscious:

> Discoverers of forgotten truth
> Or mere companions of my youth,
> All, all are in my thoughts to-night, being dead.

The foregoing is from the poem In Memory of Major Robert Gregory. There is another, Men Improve With the Years:

> But I grow old among dreams,
> A weather-worn, marble triton
> Among the streams.

One or two of the briefer poems, notably one called To a Squirrel at Kyle-na-Gno, present Yeats in the aspect of seeking to copy the simplicity, or rather the Irish naivete, of James Stephens—and doing it indifferently well. As for The Balloon of the Mind—

> Hands, do what you're bid;
> Bring the balloon of the mind
> That bellies and drags in the wind
> Into its narrow shed

—it has the gesture of Greenwich Village about it. More in the spirit of the earlier Yeats are The Phases of the Moon, with its subtly evoked images, and The Sad Shepherd, told with the poetic dignity which weaves a potent charm. Considered as a whole, however, The Wild Swans of Coole beat upon the fancy with ineffectual wings.

Reproduction of an anonymous review from *The Dial*, 1919.

Right away he insisted that he and I spend an intense period in textual analysis. There are five plays in the cycle, from the mystical in *At The Hawk's Well*, to the farcical in *The Green Helmet,* the magical in *The Only Jealousy of Emer* to the political in *On Baile's Strand* and the tragic and esoteric in *The Death of Cuchulain.* And so, over a fortnight, we sat together and went through all five plays line by line, Flannery continually highlighting layers of meaning within the text, and encouraging me to think as broadly as possible, to be as free with as many music idioms as I wished in approaching the work. And of course, in each of the plays there was also a requirement for underscoring, for dance and for ambient music where I was not impelled by the rises and falls of the text, but more by moods and colours that the director was trying to create – somewhat akin to film music.

I soon began to realize that the key into the music of Yeats's lyrics was in the very definite rhythmic pillars upon which the verses are built. Once you had stepped beneath these portals, you became acquainted with the inner music of the lines. To illustrate this, I simply opened a page at random and found an immediate example. In *The Only Jealousy of Emer,* this exquisite lyric gives a ready example of his inner music:

> A <u>wom</u>an's <u>beauty</u> is like a <u>white</u>
> <u>Frail</u> <u>bird</u>, / like a <u>white</u> <u>sea</u>-<u>bird</u> / a<u>lone</u>
> At <u>day</u>break, <u>after</u> <u>stormy</u> <u>night</u>
> Bet<u>ween</u> two <u>fur</u>rows u<u>pon</u> the <u>ploughed</u> <u>land</u> ...

The pace of these lines with the stresses I have underlined (the slashes are pauses in the rhythm) seemed to me to require a melody which was ruminative and reflective. The next line, however, totally interrupted the flow:

> A <u>sudden</u> <u>storm</u> and it was <u>thrown</u>
> Bet<u>ween</u> <u>dark</u> <u>furrows</u> upon the <u>ploughed</u> <u>land</u>.

Here I was prompted to increase the tempo of these lines to almost double the speed of the previous lines. And then it seemed totally natural to come back to the original tempo for ...

> How many centuries spent
> The sedentary soul
> In toils of measurement
> Beyond eagle or mole,
> Beyond hearing or seeing,
> Or Archimedes' guess

> To raise into being
> That loveliness.

There are many examples of these cadences in his song lyrics. Over the next five years of the festival, I wrote music for all the songs within the fifteen plays that we presented. Under Flannery's direction, I was encouraged to ignore Yeats's injunction to be monotonic, and to allow my own polyphonic response to where I found the music in the words, being careful to float the text rather than to drown it.

Whether Yeats's reputation for tone-deafness is true or not, there is no doubt that together with his acute rhythmic sensibility, he had a capacity to create an internal music that, like a river, rushed around those rhythmic rocks and rapids, and flooded the text with a rich and very particular music.

> At the grey round of the hill
> Music of a lost kingdom
> Runs, runs and is suddenly still.
> The winds out of Clare-Galway
> Carry it: suddenly it is still.
>
> I have heard in the night air
> A wandering airy music;
> And moidered in that snare
> A man is lost of a sudden,
> In that sweet wandering snare.
> — from THE DREAMING OF THE BONES

Eamon Grennan

GEARING UP

WB Yeats, *The Green Helmet and Other Poems* (Cuala Press, 1910).

It's only a decade since Mr Yeats offered to the world his *fin de siècle* wonderbook, *The Wind Among the Reeds* – a confection stuffed with such amorous delicacies, as this, from 'A Poet to His Beloved':

> I bring you with reverent hands
> The books of my numberless dreams,
> White woman that passion has worn
> As the tide wears the dove-grey sands ...

Or this, from 'He reproves the Curlew':

> O curlew, cry no more in the air,
> Or only to the water in the West;
> Because your crying brings to my mind
> Passion-dimmed eyes and long heavy hair
> That was shaken out over my breast:
> There is enough evil in the crying of wind.

Most, as we know, are love poems to his major muse Maud Gonne (as is also the brilliantly orchestrated 'The Song of Wandering Aengus,' plucking 'till time and times are done / The silver apples of the moon, / The golden apples of the sun'; Golden Delicious!). The volume also contains exquisite additions in honour of his first (as we also now know) fully consummated love affair, with his beloved, Olivia Shakespear. Hard, indeed, at times – given their prevailing dream-tinged mode – to tell the poems for Maud from those for Olivia; this one, for example:

> Had I the heavens' embroidered cloths,
> Enwrought with golden and silver light,
> The blue and the dim and the dark cloths
> Of night and light and the half-light,
> I would spread the cloths under your feet:
> But I, being poor, have only my dreams;
> I have spread my dreams under your feet;
> Tread softly because you tread on my dreams.
> – 'HE WISHES FOR THE CLOTHS OF HEAVEN'

Whomever they're for, such poems put Yeats – with Petrarch and Dante behind him, not to mention the troubadours – in the forefront of the love lyricists of his time. It was of course the poet himself who has passed judgment on their like, remarking that broody poems of this ilk were not so much the way to *win* as the way to *lose* a lady. Perhaps, but no matter. For in these rhythmically hypnotic raids on the paraphernalia of the Celtic Twilight and his own fevered heart, Yeats endeared himself to the aesthetically exquisite sensibilities of the Nineties, striking – in a more or less Irish accent – their pose, particular mood, and tone:

> Pale brows, still hands and dim hair,
> I had a beautiful friend
> And dreamed that the old despair
> Would end in love in the end ...
>   – 'THE LOVER MOURNS FOR THE LOSS OF LOVE'

After such a feast of dreams, it's a sharp wake-up call to come upon the shift of gears and change of temper (not to mention temperature) in this latest production: *The Green Helmet and Other Poems*. In what follows I'll confine myself to the 'other poems', since I'll let others pass judgment on the verse play. (The poet calls it a 'Heroic Farce' – a piece notable for the fluency of its couplets, the speed of its dramatic exchanges, and the embroidered texture of its *ambiente*). In truth, however, the play does reinforce my sense that there's something intrinsically dramatic in Yeats's lyric imagination, a *dramatic* energy that flares to life in many of these poems: in their voicings, in their sense of a man seeking a right, a convincing *speech*: to present – to enact – vexing problems (of character, of feeling, even of politics) in his own life. And it's impressive to see how he has left most of that Celtic Twilight *son et lumière* behind, and is here igniting harsher lyrical lights, letting more iron into his verse, stiffening it (both in language and feeling) toward harder, sharper, stricter poems. Here, instead of 'pale brows, still hands and dim hair' we have:

> Why should I blame her that she fill my days
> With misery, or that she would of late
> Have taught to ignorant men most violent ways,
> Or hurled the little streets upon the great,
> Had they but courage equal to desire?
>   – 'NO SECOND TROY'

Here, passionate utterance has taken over from lyric sigh; tough diction replaces plangent gesture; a turbulent daylit cityscape takes over from a twilit Romantic, dream-inflected landscape; wakeful, interrogative, polit-

ically alert human passion shakes amorous lament to its lyrical core.
There were intimations of such a shift in the collection before this one
(*In the Seven Woods*) – in a poem like 'Adam's Curse,' for example:

> 'Better go down upon your marrow-bones
> And scrub a kitchen pavement, or break stones
> Like an old pauper, in all kinds of weather;
> For to articulate sweet sounds together
> Is to work harder than all these, and yet
> Be thought an idler by the noisy set
> Of bankers, schoolmasters, and clergymen
> The martyrs call the world.'

But the best poems in *The Green Helmet* go well beyond that – in toughness
of address and in their direct confrontation with their subject matter.
Here, Pre-Raphaelite glow and gesture have given way to certain
qualities (e.g., a robust syntax) that Yeats may have learned from his study
of Donne, as well as from his recently established friendship with the
brash young American poet, Ezra Pound. Indeed it's possible to speculate
that Pound's poems (in *Personae*, published this same year) of Masks
(itself a Yeatsian notion) and Pound's urgently colloquial (if also slightly
archaic) speech could have helped to marshal Yeats the way that he was
going – towards a quickened language of direct address. Something
harder, more direct, a more performative, syntactically more supple
speech. A different sort of music. Truth is, these poems bear the mark of
a poet willing to take on cultural ambivalences and wide-awake
heartaches, a poet who – neither losing a decisively determined
rhetorical panache nor the *ritual* of form – wants to let the whole of his
life into his verse, including not only its loss of the woman he loves (a
loss that was made bitterly palpable by his muse's marriage to the
soldier-veteran of the Boer War, the nationalist Major John MacBride),
but a complementary need to express a tough, clear-headed critique of
the loved one as well:

> She lived in storm and strife,
> Her soul had such desire
> For what proud death may bring
> That it could not endure
> The common good of life ...
>   – 'THAT THE NIGHT COME'

Such directness takes the poet out of earshot of the wind that blows
among the reeds, and carries him into a more demanding world of

thought and feeling than those in which he has lyrically sojourned up to now:

> And I that have not your faith, how shall I know
> That in the blinding light beyond the grave
> We'll find so good a thing as that we have lost?
> The hourly kindness, the day's common speech,
> The habitual content of each with each
> When neither soul nor body has been crossed.
>
> — 'KING AND NO KING'

Personally, what I relish most in this collection is its achievement of raw passionate statement without loss of formal poise, a quality at its most rigorous in the unsparing self-knowledge of a poem such as 'The Cold Heaven'. Again here, the actual thinking presence of the stricken speaker is made palpable in the gathering up of elements (rhymes, rhythms, syntactically versatile iambics and all) into the magisterial assertion of an unanswerable question:

> ... Ah! when the ghost begins to quicken,
> Confusion of the death-bed over, is it sent
> Out naked on the roads, as the books say, and stricken
> By the injustice of the skies for punishment?

Such ending on an interrogative ('Was there another Troy for her to burn?') has become in this collection a strategy to allow the poet to hover above meanings, rather than deciding upon any one of them as the burden of his poem. In this way he comes at a sort of poem that keeps pace with its own making, its own discoveries. It is a fruitful, fascinating, and promising direction.

So it's especially satisfying to see the poet in this fresh collection taking on, in so many of these poems, his own conscious self and his given world – confronting them in a way that suggests a *taking responsibility: responding*, that is, in an alert, imaginatively muscular way, to his life and to the world in which it must persist. With this volume, I believe, Mr Yeats has himself stepped *responsibly* out onto a poetic road that may have many a turning and many a rich revelation before it reaches, if it ever reaches, its destination. So what can we say – with apologies to the sectarians of the Golden Dawn – except ... *Godspeed!*

WB Yeats

HE THINKS OF THOSE WHO HAVE SPOKEN EVIL OF HIS BELOVED

Half close your eyelids, loosen your hair,
And dream about the great and their pride;
They have spoken against you everywhere,
But weigh this song with the great and their pride;
I made it out of a mouthful of air,
Their children's children shall say they have lied.

Bill Manhire

MUNCH

I made it out of a mouthful of air.
Foolish balloon that bounced

from hand to hand
like a difficult

friend at a party. But you
weren't even

there, says the difficult
friend in question.

Get out of here!

You mouthful of cheese.
You morsel.

WB Yeats

A FIRST CONFESSION

I admit the briar
Entangled in my hair
Did not injure me;
My blenching and trembling
Nothing but dissembling,
Nothing but coquetry.

I long for truth, and yet
I cannot stay from that
My better self disowns,
For a man's attention
Brings such satisfaction
To the craving in my bones.

Brightness that I pull back
From the Zodiac,
Why those questioning eyes
That are fixed upon me?
What can they do but shun me
If empty night replies?

Denise Riley

I admit the briar.
The grave rose knots it
Both coiled about in shade.

A padded heart draws barbs –
Worked free, they won't make
Relics however buffed up.

Full of wist, I need not be.
The fuller world's not 'cruel' to me
More like indifferent –

I am that world. What was it
Flora Tristan cried
In her corkscrew gaiety:

'When I behold Thy crown of thorns,
Thy bitter trials, O Lord, how trivial
Do they seem compared to mine!'

Patrick McGuinness

ON THE DOUBLE

My resistance to Yeats came, like most literary resistances, from school English lessons. It was the vatic Yeats we were sold, not the national poet, but either way I wasn't interested. To someone 'carrying around' (my father's phrase) an Irish name in 1980s England, the national dimension was there, mute and irrelevant but not, for all that, completely ignored. We were taught 'An Irish Airman Foresees his Death' as a war poem, though whose war was not something we went into. The words 'country' and 'countrymen' were there, and we even discussed, in class, where Kiltartan Cross was ('somewhere in Scotland' offered my neighbour, 'obvs'), but in the context of its being a local rather than a national reference-point (rather than what it is: a national reference-point evoked through a local one).

My father's refusal to claim Irishness, or his belief that he had none, played a part in my own sense of Yeats being remote from anything that might be relevant to me. When I studied English at university, we spent too much time on poems like 'The Wanderings of Oisin' and on the occult, psycho-babbly spiritualism for me to see past the Celtic Twilight and into anything clearer. Besides, I had also discovered Dylan Thomas, who had the added attraction of being tragic and incomprehensible, and therefore of fulfilling two of poetry's primary desiderata. Even Yeats's late poems, which might have snagged my dissipated attention, seemed to dramatize the self in ways that put me off.

In the mid-1990s, I found myself on the Euston-Holyhead train, whose place in the literatures of Wales and Ireland has been brilliantly explored by Claire Connolly*. That first journey ended in Bangor for me, but now, nearly twenty years on, it's part of my weekly commute to Oxford. I've always been fascinated by rail lines – by their ongoingness, their mix of precision and chaos, the ramifying, tentacular branchings from main line to local line and back, by points changes, sidings and terminii. The whole package always seemed to me a good way of thinking about life, but also, and less of a cliché, about how literature works: how influence and enthusiasm happen and shape people and places, making up that thing we call culture. Then there is the bonus of the stations, which, in Wales as in Ireland, come bilingually, so you get them twice, seeing and hearing them double.

One specifically Yeatsian doubling came when I read RS Thomas's 'Memories of Yeats Whilst Travelling to Holyhead', while on the same train as RS Thomas was writing about. It's an early poem, 1946, and doesn't yet have the wiriness of thought and the gauntness of diction of the RS Thomas we know best. The sighting of Yeats is invented, but for the poem to work the sighting must, in a sense, not have happened. In Thomas's poem, Yeats sits in the 'indifferent compartment, hurled / Between the waves' white audience, the earth's dim screen'. The young Welsh poet is too intimidated to speak to him, but in any case Yeats has already turned away from the mountains to his left and the waves to his right, 'lost in the amazing / And labyrinth paths of his own impenetrable mind'. The poem ends with RS taking his cue from the Master, and turning inwards, or rather turning *in outwards*, towards the dream: 'I had known reality dwindle, the dream begin'.

Those of us who take that train today have little by way of dream vision. It's still a beautiful ride for scenery, though what Yeats might have called the 'turbine-torn' sea looks a little different, and there are caravan parks and out-of-town supermarkets between us and the mountains. It's also an industrial landscape, no longer separate from the rural but woven into it: rusting retired ships, a chemical plant on the English side as we head west which, shimmering on a hazy day, looks as towered and domed as Venice, the quarries sitting alongside the dilapidated resort towns – all things RS Thomas objected to, and which were part, he thought, of the Anglicisation of his country, its correlatives as well as its causes. In the compartment itself, with the out-of-order toilet, the phone ringtones, the buffet sliding like a hearse down the corridor, you can see why someone might want to turn inwards. For Thomas, the 'dream' he turns inwards to is, in large part, a nationalist one, by which I mean a cultural and culturalist rather than necessarily party-political one (though Thomas is of course extremely and fearlessly political outside his poems). The 'dream' of this Yeats-inspired poem is, I think, also where the 'responsibility' of choosing to become a national poet 'begins'. So Yeats is present, as it were, and yet not there at the birth of RS Thomas the Welsh national poet.

The Holyhead train was for Thomas also a location for confronting the different trajectories of Ireland and Wales. He was never optimistic enough (unlike Yeats) to believe fully in culture as a defining force in national struggle, but that pessimism is what makes Thomas himself. Yet that belief in Wales and Ireland being, in a more than metaphorical way, on the same line, the same track, on the same train if not the same compartment is responsible for the small glow of optimism that warms even Thomas's bleakest poetry.

My finding Yeats again comes mostly from that perspective now: a meeting that never took place between two national poets of countries I don't belong to, on a train to what is nonetheless my home: Caernarfon, a coastal town which is in its way the capital of Welsh-speaking Wales.

We are so close to Ireland that when I go to my local supermarket my phone messages me with the words 'Welcome to Ireland', and then proceeds to charge me extra. There's a poem in that, and I may yet write it.

I've been a member of Plaid Cymru since I moved to Wales, and loving RS Thomas has not dented my optimism about what lies ahead. Reading Yeats (and Thomas) in the context of devolution in the UK, of the Scottish referendum, the election results, and the impending European referendum is not to impose a temporary topical grid over their poetry, but to think about how they resonate, for good or ill, in a world that they somehow foresaw without predicting. Yeats in that sense makes me realize that Wales and Ireland are on the same train, but for now we Welsh have to get out several stops earlier.

*'Via Holyhead: Material and metaphorical meanings between Ireland and Wales' (www.ucd.ie/scholarcast/scholarcast35.html)

Neil Jordan

MAD ABSTRACT DARK

I heard Denis Donoghue give a lecture on Yeats in Trinity College, Dublin, based on his preliminary work for the definitive biography, a project from which he later departed in some kind of high dudgeon. But he talked of Yeats as a 'mage' and seemed to intend to take this aspect of his work to heart in the book that was never written. I would love to have read it, however good the two volumes by Roy Foster are, since the strange power of all of Yeats's work, from the earliest to the latest poems, seems to me to reside in an element most of us find faintly embarrassing, maybe risible and definitely resistant to everyday and logical understanding. That is his interest in magic, and not only his interest, his rather weird and suspect desire to make himself a mage, a figure with access to powers of symbol, language and understanding that were beyond rationality, and in a sense, beyond literature.

From his early interest in Madame Blavatsky-type table tappings and the Order of the Golden Dawn to his later attempts to build a philosophical-religio-mythical system in *A Vision*, and his experiments with automatic writing, there is a battle with the rational going on that only finds a parallel in the early surrealists. To compare Yeats to Max Ernst or André Breton would seem absurd, but one does encounter the same startling feeling in both, the strange entry into a world that doesn't want or demand to be fully understood, the world, probably, of dreams and images straight from dreams. I am not qualified, or academically educated enough, to elucidate all of these issues, but to me the numinous power of his later poetry in particular comes from elements that are, at some very deep level, inaccessible to rationality.

Beyond the politics, beyond the consciously dramatized personal history, beyond the adopted pose of 'national poet' there is something else. Something that has the whiff of the dark side about it, the kind of rituals you see mawkishly dramatized in Hammer horror movies, something that he took with a kind of manic or vatic seriousness, that is deeply impenetrable, but with a power above and beyond the rational. And maybe the power of this element is precisely that it resists understanding and analysis, that his symbolic system, whatever it was, with its grand historical cycles and strange mythical references, creates lines and images that can be understood differently by different people at different times. Which is why 'The Second Coming' can be quoted in so many contradictory contexts and situations; why the poem can be seen as a foreshadowing, a warning, a prophecy of practically anything.

The poem below is not one of his best known and probably not even his best. But every time I read it I get the same shiver, and cannot be sure why. I have looked at the possible references for the Dulac picture and none of them have anything like the same sense of violence, of incipient threat, of impending insanity and a strange, touching instinct to protect a loved one from some imaginary animal prowling outside.

I have read various commentaries on the poem, and they all make admirable sense. But none of them can explain why the green birds are horrible. What had Yeats got against parrots? Parrots might call and squawk, but they rarely swing. He was driven insane because of some green wing, he says. Why a wing, and why a green one?

The 'mad abstract dark' – I love the term and somehow recognize the feeling. And I know the seven Ephesian topers can be fully analysed by some dutiful academic. Someone said that he agonized for months over the phrase 'mummy wheat'. Wheat preserved in a mummy's tomb, I suppose, still able to grow, after centuries. And the poem is about change, reconditioning after the discovery of something ancient, and suddenly relevant again. But in the end we come back to those horrible green birds. No literary exegesis can explain their power. And the reason they communicate such a sense of nightmarish unease is because I genuinely don't know where they come from. We are in a dream, probably a nightmare but it's not a private one, it's a strangely familiar one and I can't be sure why. We are in the hands of someone who could tap into the commonality of dreams, a 'spirit by spirits taught to write', a mage.

ON A PICTURE OF A BLACK CENTAUR BY EDMUND DULAC

Your hooves have stamped at the black margin of the wood,
Even where horrible green parrots call and swing.
My works are all stamped down into the sultry mud.
I knew that horse-play, knew it for a murderous thing.
What wholesome sun has ripened is wholesome food to eat,
And that alone; yet I, being driven half insane
Because of some green wing, gathered old mummy wheat
In the mad abstract dark and ground it grain by grain
And after baked it slowly in an oven; but now
I bring full-flavoured wine out of a barrel found
Where seven Ephesian topers slept and never knew
When Alexander's empire passed, they slept so sound.
Stretch out your limbs and sleep a long Saturnian sleep;
I have loved you better than my soul for all my words,
And there is none so fit to keep a watch and keep
Unwearied eyes upon those horrible green birds.

John McAuliffe

BLACKOUT

William Butler Yeats, *Responsibilities: Poems and a Play* (Cuala Press, 1914).

One hundred years ago, WB Yeats was fifty. And *everywhere*. *Responsibilities* (and what an odd name for a book, a sort of prefatory grumble at what he had been forced by circumstances to write), the book that appeared in his fiftieth year, is a book that attempts to find a way out of his earlier positions, as editor, booster and poet of the Irish tradition. In some ways it is a book of wrong turns. And no wonder.

In 1914 he was an occasional dinner guest of Asquith's at 10 Downing Street while also dining with one of his predecessors, Arthur Balfour; he had received a 'Civil List' annuity in 1912 and would soon refuse the offer of a knighthood. In January he visited Wilfred Scawen Blunt in Sussex, part of a delegation which included young and old, Sturge Moore as well as Ezra Pound and Richard Aldington. He had just returned from two months lecturing across North America, mostly at universities, which is telling about his new positioning, given that his previous lecture tours had been on an Irish-American fund-raising circuit. (Patrick Pearse was drawing crowds on that circuit in 1914). Newspaper interviews are fewer but revealing: Yeats suggested that Edward Carson was a traitor to his constituency, and seemed minded to believe that Home Rule, with the prospect of a ten year referendum in the north, would resolve the national question, with no recurrence of insurrection.

One of the prices of Yeats's fame was that his peers had begun to write about him, to remember him; in the previous year memoirs by Katharine Tynan and George Moore made unauthorized use of his early letters and private conversations, respectively, to show him in an unfavourable light. This led Yeats to start writing an account of his own childhood that summer, an account which is also imbued with Yeats's changing sense of his chameleon self, or in the spirit of *Responsibilities'* plural title, his selves. Simultaneously, he became obsessed with a new lead in his psychical research, and he was as shocked as anyone when the British Army fired on a Volunteer demonstration at the end of July 1914, although it was his brother Jack who would respond artistically to that event in his painting 'Bachelor's Walk: In Memory'.

As he gathered together *Responsibilities* (which combined new poems with previous limited editions of 1913 and 1910, *Poems written in Discouragement* and *The Green Helmet*), his sense of his own position in the world was changing. As was the world around him with the outbreak of a European war in August 1914: Yeats wrote about that from a distance, wondering to one correspondent about how the war would affect the Abbey's UK tour revenue, 'how will war affect the minds of the audience it leaves us', he writes, but also: 'In Ireland we want .. a war to unite us all'. His feeling of separateness from the war was remarked on by Maud Gonne who was living in France and would work as a nurse in a field hospital there, writing to him, 'You seemed to have escaped the obsession of this war'. Yeats was in a London bank when the first Zeppelin raid occurred. The night-time black-outs appealed to him: 'No Bovril ads to be seen then', he wrote.

So, no surprise that *Responsibilities* is usually seen as an interim book, a book which shows Yeats's grasp of his modern situation but lacks the imaginative *sprezzatura* we identify with the great work which followed it. Yeats's appetite for controversy, developed during his Abbey years, is evident in its most celebrated work, the poem-ballad originally published in the *Irish Times* as 'Romance in Ireland', which declared 'Romantic Ireland's dead and gone, / It's with O'Leary in the grave.' Yeats had meant the poem as an attack on Lord Ardilaun, but when a powerful newspaper owner (a recurring figure over the last century), took the bait instead, writing to the *Irish Times* to give 'Paudeen's view' about wasting money on fancy foreign pictures, Yeats enlarged his attack to include him, so much so that he appeared on the platform of debates about the lockout later that year and a long letter of his appeared in *The Irish Worker* in late 1913.

Here, and elsewhere, Yeats seems to discover a way of using the names he was called to his own advantage. The attacks on him become a hook he baits, a way of engaging with an audience as he draws on his gift for antagonism, for offence. In his poems about art, Yeats rides his high horse into enemy territory. And maybe he was just checking that his finger was on the pulse in some of the brilliant outlier poems, which detonate in explicitly sexual ways that even now are rare in poetry: in 'On those that hated *The Playboy of the Western World*, 1907', envious men are rendered eunuch-like by Synge's Don Juan-like power: they 'rail and sweat / Staring upon his sinewy thigh'; a marriage night is to be graced by 'the outrageous cannon, / To bundle time away / That the night come' ('That the Night Come'); and 'The Magi' turn their attention 'Being by Calvary's turbulence unsatisfied, / [to] The uncontrollable mystery on the bestial floor'. (And of course it was the erotic subjects of the Hugh Lane bequest that polarized debates about housing the work in the Municipal Art Gallery).

But the antagonism of *Responsibilities* is not only sexual or political, although it is those elements which become permanent aspects of his poems' resources in later books. But it is one of the book's 'wrong turns', the long poem with which the collection begins, 'The Grey Rock', which introduces another interesting development, one which – unlike those other antagonising subjects – Yeats would not sustain in his later books. 'The Grey Rock' is the first of Yeats's poems to explicitly address an English audience. The poem's chosen interlocutors are his old poet-companions from the London pub, The Cheshire Cheese, which they frequented more than he did. Here they are, Ernest Dowson, Arthur Symons, Lionel Johnston: *'Poets with whom I learned my trade, / Companions of the Cheshire Cheese'*. How big a change is this? Yeats had addressed others – 'At the Abbey Theatre' began, 'Dear Craoibhin Aoibhin' (in 1912); 'Reconciliation' addresses Maud Gonne, 'Some may have blamed you' (1910), and 'The Lover pleads with his Friend for Old Friends' begins, 'Though you are in your shining days' (in 1897); while Ireland's future population are put *faoi gheasa* in 'To Ireland in the Coming Times' in 1892 (*'I cast my heart into my rhymes, / That you, in the dim coming times'*).

But if Yeats is choosing to address his dead English friends at the start of his new book, a book written as he moved between Dublin, the USA and, increasingly, the south of England, he is not relinquishing his right to speak of Ireland to them. The poem's subject is the Battle of Clontarf, where the supernatural Aoife is abandoned by her lover, who chooses to die for Ireland rather than to live for her. She tells her story to the gods at Slievenamon, hoping they will exercise their power to bring her beloved back. Instead, in a scene which must rank as one of Yeats's strangest, they encircle her and drench her with wine so that she forgets what has befallen her. It is a story which has a momentum of its own, but as is so usual in Yeats, on closer consideration it feels at times like a not uncritical medita-tion on the alcoholic fates of his English friends, as well as on Yeats's own feelings about friends signing up for violent nationalism.

In *Poetry,* Ezra Pound called the poem 'as obscure, at least, as [Browning's] *Sordello'* but its import and point seem clear enough when we consider that in 1915 Yeats's life of criss-crossing the Irish Sea was tilted away from Ireland to his English address, and that this is the first of his poems to draw on that bilocation, to grant his Irish and English backgrounds and audiences 'parity of esteem' in a single poem, within a single frame, imagining a changed relationship between England and Ireland: 'the world's altered since you died' he tells his former companions, which reflects Yeats's new faith in civil relations and home rule reforms on both sides of the Irish Sea.

The ending drifts back from the Cheshire Cheese and The Grey Rock, when it confidently asks its reader to choose love or war:

> And the world's altered since you died,
> And I am in no good repute

With the loud host before the sea,
That think sword-strokes were better meant
Than lover's music – let that be,
So that the wandering foot's content.

The 'wandering foot' is Yeats's, but Easter 1916 and, subsequently, 'Easter 1916' made Yeats put his foot down and re-align his poems again. None of this really affects his poems' distinctive rhythms – see the characteristic wobble of 'the wandering foot' between iambs in the last line – or his ability to push his reader's buttons if he needed to. Byzantium, Crazy Jane, the classical world would in future provide him with similar pivots, as the London pub does in 'The Grey Rock.' The poem might be said to open up cross-currents that surface occasionally afterwards, in the London poems of Kavanagh and Boland and Riordan and Heaney, in the northern England of Pearse Hutchinson, Bernard O'Donoghue and the younger generation of Irish poets who live and write there.

And as we look again at the motley, dreamy projections of *Responsibilities,* what else is there to see? Scraps of speech, which Yeats could hear and use, setting tones against one another with great dramatic force. 'Hope that you may understand!', begins 'The Realists'; '"O dear, / It was an accident"' ends 'The Dolls'. And *Responsibilities* includes one of my favourite poetic gear-changes, when *The Cold Heaven,* one of my favourite poems, runs, 'And thereupon imagination and heart' (as ponderous a pairing as Yeats ever made) to the hairpin enjambments of,

> And thereupon imagination and heart were driven
> So wild that every casual thought of that and this
> Vanished ...

... before the poem goes wild, driving further and further into areas about which little is known, mining the unknowable, alluding to Hamlet, hammering home his end-rhymes, repeating words ('all'),

> ... and left but memories, that should be out of season
> With the hot blood of youth, of love crossed long ago;
> And I took all the blame out of all sense and reason ...

... and getting so carried away that he takes us with him, away from the London blackouts, American lecture halls and Dublin art galleries where he believed 'all thought among us is frozen into something other than human life' to where, 'confusion of the death-bed over', we are with him in that place, 'Out naked on the roads ... and stricken / By the injustice of the skies for punishment'.

WB Yeats

from VACILLATION

IV

My fiftieth year had come and gone,
I sat, a solitary man,
In a crowded London shop,
An open book and empty cup
On the marble table-top.

While on the shop and street I gazed
My body of a sudden blazed;
And twenty minutes more or less
It seemed, so great my happiness,
That I was blessed and could bless.

Harry Clifton

CHEZ JEANETTE

> My fiftieth year had come and gone,
> I sat, a solitary man,
> In a crowded London shop …
> > – WB Yeats

And so do I, past fifty now,
In the gilt and mirror-glass
Of Chez Jeanette's immigrant bar.
Wine, cassis, an overflow
Spilt on the table – marble
Like Yeats' but more of a mess.

Behind the bottles on the shelf
A real, a transcendental self
Is hiding. Great Master,
Tell me, as you sat with your cup,
And grace came down like interruption,
Did these flakes of ceiling plaster

Also drown in your dregs?
The fallen angels, broken spirits
Told like tea-leaves, disinherited,
Sold into Egypt? Child-wives, pregnant,
Hide the future, keep it dark.
Splinter-groups of young Turks

Stand at the counter, arguing.
And the saucers of small change
Accumulate. The minutes, the hours,
If grace or visitation
Ever enter … A prostitute,
Bottom of the range,

Her hangdog client, middle-aged,
Go next door, to the short-time hotel.
In the hour that God alone sees,
We are all anonymities,
No-one finds us, we cannot be paged
In Dante's Heaven, Swedenborg's Hell

Or the visions of William Yeats.
And whether the hour is early or late
Or out of time, I do not know.
But for now, it comes down to this –
The marble top, the wine, cassis,
And the finite afterglow.

WB Yeats

THE WILD SWANS AT COOLE

The trees are in their autumn beauty,
The woodland paths are dry,
Under the October twilight the water
Mirrors a still sky;
Upon the brimming water among the stones
Are nine-and-fifty swans.

The nineteenth autumn has come upon me
Since I first made my count;
I saw, before I had well finished,
All suddenly mount
And scatter wheeling in great broken rings
Upon their clamorous wings.

I have looked upon those brilliant creatures,
And now my heart is sore.
All's changed since I, hearing at twilight,
The first time on this shore,
The bell-beat of their wings above my head,
Trod with a lighter tread.

Unwearied still, lover by lover,
They paddle in the cold
Companionable streams or climb the air;
Their hearts have not grown old;
Passion or conquest, wander where they will,
Attend upon them still.

But now they drift on the still water,
Mysterious, beautiful;
Among what rushes will they build,
By what lake's edge or pool
Delight men's eyes when I awake some day
To find they have flown away?

Campbell McGrath

YEATS'S SWANS

> Upon the brimming water among the stones
> Are nine-and-fifty swans.
>   – WB Yeats

On the seldom-visited, west-looking, wave-etched headland,
the ancient fortress buried in high grass has softened
into barrow mounds grazed by sheep,

its tumbled stones claimed by farmers across generations
to enclose their pastures in drystone walls
stitched like rough sutures across a quilt of green fields,

and the government has built a new lighthouse
beside the old castle
from which the beacon signals

like a jewel refracting sunlight from the mind's tower
and the sea reflects back
its prismatic imagination of the future.

So time is not a god but a golden mirror,
an aspect of self-consciousness,
the frenzy of swans settling to water.

And when they insinuate their snakelike necks
below the surface what
can they perceive of the afterlife?

And when a fish breaches suddenly, leaping free
of its element, crossing over
to the suffocating, planar emptiness of our world,

is this not what visionaries see?
Is this heaven, then,
this voluptuous, sun-stricken, gravity-ridden realm?

And afterward, to fall back
from such a height,
to surrender celestial fire for common salt.

The birds on the water resemble sleepwalkers now
and our words clatter like stones
on a shore slipping from sunlight into shadow.

Soon the wild swans are far behind, and Sligo's silver loom
of waves is far behind us,
and the cottage-clotted hackles of the *gaeltacht*

as the road which has risen from fens to treeless moors
vanishes into the ambiguous light of eternity
beneath the ash-draggled slopes of Mount Errigal.

WB Yeats

NO SECOND TROY

Why should I blame her that she filled my days
With misery, or that she would of late
Have taught to ignorant men most violent ways,
Or hurled the little streets upon the great,
Had they but courage equal to desire?
What could have made her peaceful with a mind
That nobleness made simple as a fire,
With beauty like a tightened bow, a kind
That is not natural in an age like this,
Being high and solitary and most stern?
Why, what could she have done, being what she is?
Was there another Troy for her to burn?

Nell Regan

SCHEME

Why should I blame her that she filled my days
with colour? With neutrals that work well
on walls; Cold Dawn, Pavement Grey,
Borrowed Light® and Pearl-pale.
What would make our island unit sing?
I saw Linnets' Wing or Burnished Dove
but yielded soon to Helmet Green –
it did offset the Silver Apple of our stove.
But that was then. This is now. More
Charred Troy than Hammered Gold, we're cut
to the Hare-bone White of our
lives. All is utterly repossessed.

Note: 'Borrowed Light' is the registered name of a Farrow & Ball paint. All
other colours come from the special commemorative range 'Poet's Palette'.

WB Yeats

TO THE ROSE UPON THE ROOD OF TIME

Red Rose, proud Rose, sad Rose of all my days!
Come near me, while I sing the ancient ways:
Cuchulain battling with the bitter tide;
The Druid, grey, wood-nurtured, quiet-eyed,
Who cast round Fergus dreams, and ruin untold;   5
And thine own sadness, whereof stars, grown old
In dancing silver-sandalled on the sea,
Sing in their high and lonely melody.
Come near, that no more blinded by man's fate,
I find under the boughs of love and hate,   10
In all poor foolish things that live a day,
Eternal beauty wandering on her way.

Come near, come near, come near – Ah, leave me still
A little space for the rose-breath to fill!
Lest I no more hear common things that crave;   15
The weak worm hiding down in its small cave,
The field-mouse running by me in the grass,
And heavy mortal hopes that toil and pass;
But seek alone to hear the strange things said
By God to the bright hearts of those long dead,   20
And learn to chaunt a tongue men do not know.
Come near; I would, before my time to go,
Sing of old Eire and the ancient ways:
Red Rose, proud Rose, sad Rose of all my days.

Thomas Kinsella

TWO PERSONAL READINGS FROM *THE ROSE* (1893).

TO THE ROSE UPON THE ROOD OF TIME

Title: An address to the Rose, the essence of timeless beauty, a beauty confined in temporal matter and suffering amongst us;

ll. 1/2: beauty that has been the concern of the poet's life and work; red for its beauty as of the worldly rose, proud for its completeness, and sad for the use that has been made of it. A call to come close and listen to his song, as he sings of things remote in time.

ll. 3/5: His first ancient theme: details from the Ulster cycle, in its fantasy version.

ll. 6/8: A second theme: the Rose's own sadness, as in line 1; sung in high and lonely melody, not by the poet but by the stars – themselves worn by time, and in words appropriate to the Rose's sadness, but which are acceptable to the reader for their verbal beauty and not for any distinct meaning – stars 'silver-sandalled'.

ll. 9/12: The call to the Rose repeated: to approach and clear the poet's eyes of the merely human and let him see the timeless beauty beneath man's condition and emotions (envisioned briefly as a tree – the rood of time) and in the substance of all things ephemeral.

ll. 13/15: The call urgently repeated – but with a caution: to come close, but not yet …To leave a space for him to sing of the temporal world and its detail before he sings only of the Rose.

ll. 16/18: Examples of his earthly concerns: at one extreme, two tiny creatures; at the other, the hopes and efforts of all mankind.

ll. 19/21: And at a possibly great cost, if the Rose were to come too soon: failure in his art – chanting, alone, in occult language, and not singing to men

ll. 22/24: – a possibility that was part of the reason for his call, and for the existence of the poem.

WB Yeats

TO IRELAND IN THE COMING TIMES

Know, that I would accounted be
True brother of a company
That sang, to sweeten Ireland's wrong,
Ballad and story, rann and song;
Nor be I any less of them,   5
Because the red-rose-bordered hem
Of her, whose history began
Before God made the angelic clan,
Trails all about the written page.
When Time began to rant and rage   10
The measure of her flying feet
Made Ireland's heart begin to beat;
And Time bade all his candles flare
To light a measure here and there;
And may the thoughts of Ireland brood   15
Upon a measured quietude.

Nor may I less be counted one
With Davis, Mangan, Ferguson,
Because, to him who ponders well,
My rhymes more than their rhyming tell   20
Of things discovered in the deep,
Where only body's laid asleep.
For the elemental creatures go
About my table to and fro,
That hurry from unmeasured mind   25
To rant and rage in flood and wind;
Yet he who treads in measured ways
May surely barter gaze for gaze.
Man ever journeys on with them
After the red-rose-bordered hem.   30
Ah, faeries, dancing under the moon,
A Druid land, a Druid tune!

TO IRELAND IN THE COMING TIMES

Title, and ll. 1/4: An address to his future audience in Ireland, wanting to be counted among the folk poets whose songs and poems helped to make bearable the country's long period of oppression. With no apparent thought, on his part, of participating with them in their concerns ...

ll. 5/9: ... but asking not to be refused on account of his other high concerns, with the world before Paradise and its 'clan' of angels, and with the essence of a Beauty that existed, 'unmeasured', before the creation of Time.

ll. 10/12: At the creation of Time, introducing 'measure', order and rhythm – and anger – into the world, Beauty remained still in existence. So that She was there at the creation of Ireland. Beauty, therefore, and the poet's concern with Beauty in his song, are not irrelevant to Ireland.

ll. 13/14: Time, despite its initial anger, responded to Beauty and to the order of the dance; finding its own order and measure;

ll. 15/16: a prayer that Ireland, with all its wrongs, will respond likewise, in an ordered peace.

ll. 17/22: The argument particularized, with the naming of three of Ireland's poets (of whom only Davis might be thought directly concerned with Ireland's wrongs) ...

ll. 23/24: ... and with the details of the poet's own process of artistic creation: the first stage, with the timeless entities of his subject matter alive all about his table...

ll. 25/26: ... as they emerge, unmeasured, from 'the deep' of his mind to take their places – furious initially as they encounter Time...

ll. 27/28: ... then brought to order, in the dance of Beauty, by the poet engaging them eye to eye.

ll. 29/30: Mankind and the temporal now transformed; together with the elemental – and transformed – pre-Paradisal world. All journeying together ...

ll. 31/32: ...toward a destined end; the end not specified, but with all the features of a folk Irish world.

While still I may, I write for you
The love I lived, the dream I knew.
From our birthday, until we die,   35
Is but the winking of an eye;
And we, our singing and our love,
What measurer Time has lit above,
And all benighted things that go
About my table to and fro,   40
Are passing on to where may be,
In truth's consuming ecstasy,
No place for love and dream at all;
For God goes by with white footfall.
I cast my heart into my rhymes,   45
That you, in the dim coming times,
May know how my heart went with them
After the red-rose-bordered hem.

ll. 33/36: The poet writing, during his brief lifetime, of both realities: of earthly love and the dream;

ll. 37/44: of the temporal and the elemental journeying together – as in ll. 29/30 – toward an end now more clearly imagined: a world of divine truth that will consume all things in the ecstasy of its fire.

ll. 45/48: The address to his future audience explained in this way and brought to an end: his heart and song, even though dealing with Beauty and the other world, are concerned as much, therefore, with the affairs of Ireland and the temporal world.

The subject simple: the wish to be accepted as a poet of this world, in particular of Ireland, despite his preoccupation with things of the other world. The poet accepts that there is a special difficulty in relation to his position in the Irish poetic tradition, and the address is uneasy. It is an excuse more than an explanation, a syllogism to save him from having to deal directly with current Irish matters.

Writers in an integral society do not need to ask for special allowances in subject matter from their audience. Ireland, in this sense, is not an integral society; it uses an imported vernacular, and inherits a divided tradition, the outcome of colonial settlement. Yeats, of Irish birth and origin, had established himself early in London and made himself part of the English literary and publishing scene. It is on this basis, as an Anglo-Irish poet, that he is asking his future Irish audience to accept him, with all his mystic concerns, in company with the Irish poets of the past who wrote for them as an oppressed people.

The poem has an additional purpose. Placed at the end of *The Rose*, the book containing 'The Man who Dreamed of Faeryland', 'The Lake Isle of Innisfree', with 'Old Eire' and the figures of Fergus and Cuchulain presented in a light softened for easy acceptance, it is meant to be overheard by Yeats's English audience as he establishes himself among them, while distinguishing himself from them on the basis of subject matter.

Peter Fallon

ORDERING A NEW WORLD

WB Yeats, *The Wild Swans at Coole* (Macmillan and Co, 1919).

The Wild Swans at Coole, priced at 6 shillings, is the first collection of new
poems by William Butler Yeats since he sounded a radical tone in
Responsibilities, published five years ago. In the intervening period the
Great War that began in the year of that book's publication has run its
awful course. The Easter Rising advanced from bold aspiration to
historical fact and Ireland, in its search and struggle for self-determination,
remains an agitated land. The author of this large, wide-ranging volume
remains a key figure in the forging of an independent Irish identity. In
the post-War new world order, the new Ireland he has helped to imagine
suddenly appears to be within touching distance.

So, as the collection comes before us, what can we say of the world
order of poetry and other writings? The doleful influence of Tennyson
has continued, inevitably, to weaken. Robert Frost, a young American,
has registered his own new notes in the riddling beauties of 'Birches' and
'The Road Not Taken' in *Mountain Interval* (1916). TS Eliot, another
American abroad, announced his elusive, cosmopolitan interests in
Prufrock and Other Observations (1917) and in his *Poems* published this year.
Ezra Pound followed his performances of transliteration from the
Chinese of Li Po in *Cathay* (1915) by flexing further imaginative muscles
in a continuing excavation of tradition, mining the Provençal, Italian,
Old English and other poetries as epitomized by 'Homage to Sextus
Propertius' in *Quia Pauper Amavi*, also published this year. The elder
English novelist, Thomas Hardy, has published several volumes of verses
which have been, thus far, less warmly received than his deeply
atmospheric 'Wessex' tales. In other writing, in the wake of his *Dubliners*
(1914), *A Portrait of the Artist as a Young Man* (1916) and last year's play,
Exiles, who can imagine what Joyce is doing? The deaths of the English
poets Edward Thomas, Rupert Brooke and Wilfred Owen, casualties all
of the long brutal war, have stilled talents touched by promise (and
perhaps, in the case of Owen, genius), while the recent death, not yet
thirty, of our own 'Blackbird', Francis Ledwidge, on the blood-drenched
fields of Flanders intensified sore loss in the knowledge that his voice
will sing no more. Austin Clarke's *The Vengeance of Fionn* (1917) shows
him still at sea in the narrative retellings of ancients sagas, while Padraic
Colum has taken his quaint lyrics with him to America.

As the author notes in his Preface, written at Ballylee in Co Galway in
September of last year, *The Wild Swans at Coole* is in part a reprint of a

collection printed 'a year ago on my sister's hand-press, at Dundrum, Co Dublin'. It omits a play included in that volume and adds even more recent poems. This handsome edition is presented in Macmillan's distinctive livery, a blue cloth binding, gold embossed with Sturge Moore's spare, striking design of lines and fitting motifs. In the book's generous font and leading it is an excitement to hear, and to be addressed by, a voice so clear, convincing and compelling, the first of such authority since the revolutionary work of *Lyrical Ballads* a century ago. On the evidence of his previous collection and of certain poems in this book Yeats is the greatest poet alive.

The book, marked by rue and regret, comprises thirty-nine poems and a work in seven sections, 'Upon a Dying Lady'. There are 'Lines Written in Dejection' as well as elegies – for Major Robert Gregory, son of his friend and collaborator, and for Alfred Pollexfen, a relative who died twenty-five years ago. The book contains recognizable devices – the hallmarks of a style (such as refrains that culminate in questions) – familiar themes (controversies of political, literary and artistic nature), striking rhymes of sound *and meaning* ('Uncivil / evil') and of inventive lines ('because she is lying there' / 'we may vie with her'), vivid images ('rouge on the pallor of her face' from 'Upon a Dying Lady'), and technically subtle rhyme schemes (the recurrence of *abc* stanzas build an intriguing delay in the ear's echo chamber; see 'The Hawk'). There is evidence of a mastery of rhythm and its surprise in patterns of lines of fixed length (usually tetrameter) invigorated by variations on it:

> The trees are in their autumn beauty,
> The woodland paths are dry,
> Under the October twilight the water
> Mirrors the still sky ...
>   – 'THE WILD SWANS AT COOLE'

The book opens with undoubtable masterpieces. In the title poem's simple declarative syntax and sentences we gain the impression of a man taking notes of his observations, thinking aloud and talking both to himself and to us. If one way of comprehending the lyric poem and its form is as a frame that might surround either a window or a mirror, there's a sense here of the poet, now in his fifties, in the autumn of a year and the fading summer of his life, paying attention to a scene and concentrating it in his thought. If we imagine this is as through a window we picture him also seeing himself in the pane's reflection. The quiet reflection, in that word's other sense, contrasts with the memory of the swan's 'clamorous wings'. Between the poet's earlier light step and his heavier footfall now, the poem perfectly measures a 'hereness' with an almost prophetic, exquisite anticipation of absence or abandonment.

The astonishing inclusiveness of the author's tone or voice enlivens also the longer poem which follows. Though its title suggests the commemoration of one person, 'In Memory of Major Robert Gregory' prompts the remembrance of several. The repetition of the last word of the poem's opening stanzas, 'all ... being dead', 'are dead', knells a hammer blow of recognition.

The book's most common and dominating word is 'passion'. Yeats celebrates Synge whom he admired and encouraged for his 'passionate and simple heart'. Among his contemplations of new shades the value of passion is a recurrent touchstone. The adjective 'breathless' casts a chill on his thoughts. Death, a 'discourtesy', ultimately renders him dumb. 'An Irish Airman Foresees His Death' shares with another poem, 'The Fisherman', the verbs 'love' and 'hate' within a single couplet. But the first of these poems is consistently, and insistently, quiet. Could that 'lonely impulse' involve a suicidal inclination?

The book's central poem is the aforementioned 'The Fisherman' in which Yeats maintains in opposition and in equilibrium the portrait of an idealized figure in a western landscape with a picture of the real citizenry of a capital city, re-enacting the rage of 'September 1913' and extending the state of the nation address he launched in 'To Ireland in the Coming Times' when he was not yet thirty. In the honesty of this utterance he may be said to be writing without a mask. The poem's rhythms reverberate through our very consciousness:

> The beating down of the wise
> And great Art beaten down.

The abundant variety of the book is guaranteed by the inclusion of four dialogues. In the first of these, an eclogue that reprises the traditional form in a way that is at odds with the modernity of the book's best poems, Yeats pitches the old knowledge of the Goatherd against the simpler knowing, superstition even, of the Shepherd. The intention and process of these poems in which the poet revives figures he introduced in early stories, Michael Robartes and Owen Ahern, is to play out that 'phantasmagoria in which (he) endeavours to explain (his) philosophy of life and death'. The debate in 'The Phases of the Moon' is bookended by references to a light in a neighbouring tower that is on at first and then goes off. The seemingly random free flight, or free fall, of thought in this piece fails to 'sing / The strange reward of all that discipline'. Though overwrought, these small dramas include moments of argument, enlightenment and instruction:

A style is found by sedentary toil
And by the imitation of great masters.
— 'EGO DOMINUS TUUS'

The Wild Swans at Coole abounds with potent poems. Inevitably there are several that operate at a lower voltage than this poet has demonstrated and displayed with such panache. See 'His Phoenix' which has the look of a mere exercise. Or 'Broken Dreams' ('There is grey in your hair ...') which dissolves into nostalgia, or 'To a Squirrel at Kyle-na-gno' whose simple charm can't rescue it from sentimentality.

In the years to come the finest of these beautiful poems will melt, no doubt, into what will be the author's monumental *Collected Poems*. It will be useful and refreshing to remember that they saw their first light among the other poems and dialogues that comprise this remarkable collection. In a century's time they will be models of their form. They will last as long as language itself. It will be interesting indeed to see what this magisterial poet conjures next.

WB Yeats

For one throb of the artery,
While on that old grey stone I sat
Under the old wind-broken tree,
I knew that One is animate,
Mankind inanimate phantasy.

Rosanna Warren

LAKE STORM

For one throb of the artery, I believed
the goddess held sway and was no friend of ours.
Her cloud veils dropped, she sat enthroned.
Her silver mesh carpet shuddered across the water.
Her lions heaved, thudded, and hissed
against the stones, flashing claws of foam.
No wall would hold them. We hadn't made
the sacrifices or said the words.
My moon-shadow paced home beside me, kissed me good-night.

WB Yeats

BEAUTIFUL LOFTY THINGS

Beautiful lofty things: O'Leary's noble head;
My father upon the Abbey stage, before him a raging crowd:
'This Land of Saints', and then as the applause died out,
'Of plaster Saints'; his beautiful mischievous head thrown back.
Standish O'Grady supporting himself between the tables
Speaking to a drunken audience high nonsensical words;
Augusta Gregory seated at her great ormolu table,
Her eightieth winter approaching: 'Yesterday he threatened my life.
I told him that nightly from six to seven I sat at this table,
The blinds drawn up'; Maud Gonne at Howth station waiting a train,
Pallas Athene in that straight back and arrogant head:
All the Olympians; a thing never known again.

Philip Schultz

THE BOOKS OF DEAD FRIENDS

Beautiful lofty things on our shelves,
waiting to be remembered. Hold one,
run your fingers over broken spines,
splintering covers, feel the heft of
ancient cities, conquests, superb defeats,
all the blessings and curses of dreams
they dreamed together. They know,
I think, they've been abandoned,
no one else will be as incredulous, in awe.
Children whose only wish is to please,
yes, indeed, such beautiful lofty things,
rowdy, quaint and diffident. A sacrilege,
trespassing on the thoughts, intimacy
of voyages loved now a little less.

WB Yeats

AN IRISH AIRMAN FORESEES HIS DEATH

I know that I shall meet my fate
Somewhere among the clouds above;
Those that I fight I do not hate,
Those that I guard I do not love;
My country is Kiltartan Cross,
My countrymen Kiltartan's poor,
No likely end could bring them loss
Or leave them happier than before.
Nor law, nor duty bade me fight,
Nor public men, nor cheering crowds,
A lonely impulse of delight
Drove to this tumult in the clouds;
I balanced all, brought all to mind,
The years to come seemed waste of breath,
A waste of breath the years behind
In balance with this life, this death.

Martina Evans

THE IRISH AIRMAN PARACHUTES TO EARTH

> For wisdom is the property of the dead,
> A something incompatible with life; and power,
> Like everything that has the stain of blood,
> A property of the living...
>   – from 'Blood and the Moon', WB Yeats

I know that I shall meet my fate
somewhere near the ground.
Perhaps the basement where
I sleep now. I can't see
the moon there except in June
when it rides so low I put
my two rough gardening hands
on the window frame, peering
out to the left where it appears
between two buildings and I can't
decide if it's flashing a signal
or trying to hide.
The cats circle me, in courtly fashion
leaping in and out through
the green curtains onto the sill,
specially softened for them
with pink and grey Mexican blankets.
Their pupils fill with black to allow
more light while the roses glow white
over the crepuscular giant shadows
of the castor oil plant.
I don't think the cats look at the moon.
I think they just happen to glance
in that general direction.
All they want is to be told –
like my father told his cats
with his rough hand,
the light touch of his crooked fingers on their fur –
that they are not alone,
that they are important,
as for being wise,
it's hard to be sure.
Even cats are surprised into falling,
fooled by shadows
blindsided.

Margaret Mills Harper

YEATS QUIZ

1. Yeats's formal education included which institution?
   a)   Trinity College, Dublin
   b)   University of Oxford
   c)   Metropolitan School of Art
   d)   Royal Irish Academy of Music

2. Which quotation is not from Yeats?
   a)   'God has not died for the white heron.'
   b)   'Some moralist or mythological poet
        Compares the solitary soul to a swan;
        I am satisfied with that ...'
   c)   'The bird would cease and be as other birds
        But that he knows in singing not to sing.
        The question that he frames in all but words
        Is what to make of a diminished thing.'
   d)   'O honey-bees,
        Come build in the empty house of the stare.'

3. Which of the following female figures is not a veiled reference to
   Maud Gonne?
   a)   Helen of Troy
   b)   The Queen of Sheba
   c)   'a young girl, and she had the walk of a queen'
   d)   'Her present image floats into the mind'

4. Which of the following tried (without much success) to teach Yeats
   golf?
   a)   Stanley Baldwin
   b)   John McCormack
   c)   Fred Perry
   d)   Bertie Smyllie

5. Which of the following lines is not repeated in the poem in which
   it appears?
   a)   'A terrible beauty is born.'
   b)   'The silver apples of the moon, / The golden apples of the sun.'
   c)   *'The solid man and the coxcomb.'*
   d)   *'"What then?" sang Plato's ghost, "what then?"'*

6. Which of the following is also a tarot card, signifying major change and disruption of life?
a) The Green Helmet
b) The Winding Stair
c) The Tower
d) A Full Moon

7. We know Yeats joined the Hermetic Order of the Golden Dawn in 1890, but which of these organisations was he not a member of?
a) The Irish Republican Brotherhood
b) The Rhymers' Club
c) The GAA
d) The Ghost Club

8. Which metaphor is not used to describe one of the central symbols of *A Vision*?
a) a double cone
b) an hour glass
c) the great X
d) a funnel

9. Which writers have used quotations from Yeats as titles of books?
a) Eudora Welty
b) Chinua Achebe
c) Cormac McCarthy
d) All of the above

10. Which number is not significant in the poem 'The Wild Swans at Coole'?
a) Thirteen
b) Nineteen
c) Five
d) Nine-and-fifty

11. What book did Yeats buy with part of the money from his Nobel Prize?
a) Joyce's *Ulysses*
b) Balzac's *La Comédie humaine*
c) Stephen MacKenna's translation of the *Enneads* of Plotinus
d) Douglas Ainslie's translation of Benedetto Croce's *Logic as the Science of the Pure Concept*

12. To celebrate his Nobel Prize win, Yeats famously cooked up what?
a)   Irish stew
b)   Porridge
c)   Crème brûlée
d)   Sausages

13. To which violent conflict do each of the following lines refer?
a)   'Those that I fight I do not hate, / Those that I guard I do not love'.
b)   'Was it needless death after all?'.
c)   'We ... / Who are but weasels fighting in a hole'.
d)   'And maybe what they say is true / Of war and war's alarms'.

14. Who selected the poems by Yeats that were included in *The Oxford Book of Modern Verse* he edited in 1936?
a)   Ezra Pound
b)   TS Eliot
c)   George Yeats
d)   WB Yeats

15. Which of the following women was not one of Yeats's lovers?
a)   Florence Farr
b)   Olivia Shakespear
c)   Maud Gonne
d)   Annie Horniman

16. Late in his life, Yeats wrote that in response to a question someone asked him at a lecture, he came up with a list of four writers that 'most move me'. What is that list?
a)   Homer, Dante, Shelley, Blake
b)   Shakespeare, *The Arabian Nights*, William Morris, Balzac
c)   Sophocles, Synge, Raftery, Lady Gregory
d)   The Upanishads, Homer, Spenser, anonymous balladeers

Answers on page 200

Bernard O'Donoghue

THE LIVING STREAM

WB Yeats, *Michael Robartes and the Dancer* (Cuala Press, 1921).

If TS Eliot was right when he described Yeats as 'one of those few whose history is the history of their own time, who are part of the consciousness of an age which cannot be understood without them', we might go on to ask when exactly that came to be true of Yeats. There are great technical virtues in the volumes up to *Responsibilities* in 1914, but it could be claimed that it was only from the publication of *The Wild Swans at Coole* in 1919 that Yeats really became a major spokesperson for his times, in poems like 'In Memory of Major Robert Gregory' and 'An Irish Airman Foresees his Death'. Even in that volume the prevailing subject is not primarily focused on the history of the time.

Most people asked to nominate Yeats's most crucial political or historical poems would include 'Easter 1916', which is inevitably associated by Yeats with two other 1916 poems, 'Sixteen Dead Men' and 'The Rose Tree' (as well as the slightly different 'On a Political Prisoner' about Constance Markiewicz whose execution was commuted because she was a woman). We know that 'Easter 1916' was written in that year, but it was first published by Yeats in *The New Statesman* in the week of the death of Terence MacSwiney in October 1920, before its publication now in 1921. What is clear is that all three 1916 poems, having been written at the latest by April 1917, were available for inclusion in *The Wild Swans at Coole* in 1919. Yeats has deliberately held them back for inclusion in *Michael Robartes and the Dancer*, in 1921.

There are other major poems in this volume: major historical poems, indeed, including 'The Second Coming' – arguably Yeats's most important historical poem of all, even if it is history in a rather different sense. It could be claimed I think that *Michael Robartes and the Dancer*, a relatively short volume, contains a higher *proportion* of major poems than any volume by Yeats; as well as the poems already mentioned, 'A Prayer for my Daughter' follows 'The Second Coming'. But the volume in 1921, given that it has a decidedly historical bent, has a strange beginning. As well as coming to a stronger sense of history after the volume *Responsibilities*, Yeats has also concentrated more on the numinous (or the occult or the mystical: whatever word is used for what Yeats called the great concern of his life). In *Michael Robartes and the Dancer*, there are four poems from that area before the bombshell of 'Easter 1916', beginning with the title-poem in which the invented visionary Robartes (associated, it is suggested, with Yeats's mystical friend AE, George Russell) argues with the very feminine figure of the Dancer, based on Iseult Gonne, about the meaning of 'St George and the Dragon', an altarpiece in the Dublin National Gallery attributed to Bordone. It begins 'Opinion is not worth a rush', but turns quickly in a very different direction. It seems to return to the theme of 'Adam's Curse' in 1901: the Tiresian question whether women's 'labour to be beautiful' is more or less exacting than the poet's task of spending hours to compose a line which will seem 'a moment's thought'. The dragon is the lady's thought which causes her, in its opinionated way, to argue with her lover. The dancer asks, reasonably enough, 'must no beautiful woman be / Learned like a man?' Robartes's answers are inconclusive, not to say evasive.

At the end of the volume, 'A Prayer for my Daughter', the last major poem in the collection – which is concluded by two lightweight squibs, 'A Meditation in Time of War' and the dedication-plaque to Thoor Ballylee, 'I, the poet William Yeats', etc. – returns memorably to the question of opinion:

> An intellectual hatred is the worst,
> So let her think opinions are accursed.

So what has become of the decidedly opinionated and clear pronouncements in the 1916 poems here? 'Easter 1916', for example, where the mockery of the vivid, political faces of the start, is changed utterly to another plaque at the end: the naming of the revolutionaries and the terrible beauty to which they gave birth:

> MacDonagh and MacBride
> And Connolly and Pearse ...

The possibility is raised in the middle of the poem that their sacrifice has been too great: that their single, opinionated purpose has been 'Enchanted to a stone / To trouble the living stream' which is the principle of life and movement. But this reservation has been dispelled by the end and the concluding line is 'A terrible beauty is born'. The excitement of that conclusion is reinforced in the collection by the continuing in all his arrangements of the poems with 'Sixteen Dead Men' and 'The Rose Tree'.

So what are we to learn from Yeats: from Yeats at his best, as in much of this volume? One of Yeats's great appreciators and successors – what Yeats in 1908 in the poem 'At Galway Races' called 'Hearers and hearteners of the work' – Seamus Heaney said Yeats's great creative virtue was his capacity for change: to complete one subject and move to something completely different. Yeats also – not uniquely – said of some proposition 'The contrary of this is also true'. And what we also see in this volume is something that has been said to be Yeats's greatest strength: the ability to live and write in doubt. In that sense he did believe that 'Opinion is not worth a rush'. In *Michael Robartes and the Dancer* we find woven together the obscurities of Yeats's recondite system ('That blest souls are not composite' and the like), with the grim physical reality of war and death as it affected the executed 1916 leaders. It might have been logical to argue in 'Sixteen Dead Men' that Ireland should postpone Home Rule:

> Till Germany's overcome;
> But who is there to argue that
> Now Pearse is deaf and dumb?
> And is their logic to outweigh
> MacDonagh's bony thumb?

It is an extraordinary intermingling of themes and languages and obsessions. Yeats has said 'I am no nationalist, except in Ireland for passing reasons'. But by the time he has completed this volume, Yeats is ready to embark on the great political and visionary subjects: the end of the Irish War of Independence which will end in a terrible Civil War. 'They say such different things at school', the dancer says to Michael Robartes. This beautifully structured short volume – almost certainly the greatest that Yeats has written up to this point – culminates, as I have said, in a history poem that takes an extraordinarily long perspective. What exactly is threatened in 'The Second Coming'? What is the 'rough beast' that is slouching towards Bethlehem to displace Christianity? What does it presage for the new century that is just getting into its stride in January 1919? The Russian Revolution and the Irish Rebellion have happened and old certainties have been swept away. The opening image expresses this wonderfully: 'things fall apart', and the falcon is no longer within range of his master. There is a suggestion of repression to the threat felt in 'mere anarchy'; but by the end of the poem, the closing sentence hovers between statement and question:

> ... now I know
> [...]
> what rough beast, its hour come round at last,
> Slouches towards Bethlehem to be born?

It is a perfect statement of doubt: a declaration of what I know, ending with a question-mark. This is the volume in which Yeats manages to bring together declarative statement – 'A terrible beauty is born' – with personal, family-based anguish:

And for an hour I have walked and prayed
Because of the great gloom that is in my mind.
— 'A PRAYER FOR MY DAUGHTER'

There is a sense too of the unknown and mystical. Yeats has not brought these things together before this volume.

Putting these things together, we can see what Eliot so much admired. Eccentric as his thought was in many ways, Yeats fused the imaginative power of that eccentricity with the historical facts of his time in *Michael Robartes and the Dancer*. The volume's opening does not lead us to expect a powerful series of poems on political subjects; but an important part of Yeats's genius was to bring these things together in a way that expressed what Eliot called 'the consciousness of the age' as the world struggled to come to terms with new landscapes – geographical, political and philosophical.

Mary Costello

SIGNS AND SYMMETRIES

According to an endnote in the first volume of Roy Foster's biography of
WB Yeats, the poet was sighted at Athenry train station on the 7
September 1907 on his way to Coole Park for the autumn. My grandmother
was seven in 1907, and Athenry was – and still is – the family's local town.
I like to imagine she was there that day, in from the country with her
mother to do the shopping or to collect hatchery chicks off the Galway
train. It is not beyond the bounds of possibilities that, at some stage
during the thirty or more years that Yeats was coming to Coole and
Ballylee, her path crossed with his. So I play with the conceit and place
her on the platform that day, stealing glances at the tall man in the bow
tie who briefly meets her eye before turning away and resuming again
the habit of 'drifting hither and thither that must come before all true
thought and emotion'.
     Yeats was the first poet who had agency over me. In my first year at
college, the needle of my literary compass settled firmly on him. On
winter nights in the upstairs bedroom of a redbrick house on the north
side of Dublin, I fell hard for the man and the work. I'd have to haul
myself from the depths of his visions and stagger downstairs to my
housemates, a little shaken, a little dazed. At weekends I travelled west
on the train to Athenry, gazing out at the central plain, the church spires
of midland towns, the forestry cottages at Woodlawn – the same
landmarks that Yeats had gazed upon eight decades earlier. I had no
thoughts of being a writer then, but poetry had alerted me to something
– the possibility of living inwardly – and given me a glimpse of what
Rilke called 'the storming of the spirit'. I was doing what all readers do
too – trying to draw from art those experiences that closely paralleled
my own. There was little in Yeats's life that paralleled mine, but he had
once lived only a half hour's drive from my home. He must have
wandered the medieval streets of Athenry, walked under the Norman
arch on North Gate Street, past the front door of my piano teacher's
house on Church Street. I clutched at this connection and amplified it, so
that now even the swans that came to winter on our turlough no longer
recalled the Children of Lir but the nine-and-fifty above in Coole. I was
searching for affinity, looking for meaningful signs and symmetries to
make the lofty local. I was trying to reconcile my lack of literary
pedigree with what my encounters with literature were now affording
me – moments of revelation, the deepening of thought – and the
intuition that something else was being transmitted: some imaginative

possibilities that I hankered after but which might set me apart from those around me. Yeats wasn't the only writer who alerted me to these possibilities but he was the one with the closest geographical connection to home, the one in whom the literary overlapped with the local. Somewhere in that overlap, in that interface between worlds, I found my creative point of entry.

Over the years, Yeats's premier place in my poetic affections has been variously eclipsed by Eliot, Rilke, Hughes, Mahon and others. But the genius of the work and the earnestness of the life – the search for philosophical wisdom, the endless toil to awaken the imagination of a nation – constantly summon me back. And the openness, too – what Saul Bellow called the 'eternal naïveté' that a writer cannot afford to lose. With his mix of arrogance and innocence – masked man, naked self, vainglorious fool – Yeats left himself touchingly exposed.

Another September then. The morning of 17 September 1948 was bright and sunny as the LÉ *Macha*, bearing Yeats's remains home from France, docked in Galway harbour. The city's bells tolled and people lined the streets as the cortège drove out of the town and into the country, passing through Claregalway, Ballindine, Claremorris and on to Sligo.

The road from Galway to Sligo also passes through Tuam, along what is now the N17. In September 1948 my grandmother had three sons boarding at St Jarlath's College in Tuam. September the seventeenth was a Friday. Say she was in from the country bringing them fresh laundry or money for a visit to the doctor or dentist that day. Say she had just turned a corner when the cortège came into view. Her sons, inside the walls of St Jarlath's, heads bent over the *Odyssey* or *Aeneid*, might have known of the repatriation of the poet's remains, but it's unlikely that she did, as she came on the procession and was stopped short, briefly arrested by the sight of the hearse, the dignitaries inside cars, the funereal air, before recovering herself again and hurrying off on her errands.

Why am I still doing this? Shuttling back and forth across time, making dubious connections between unlinked lives? Maybe because part of the creative impulse involves making what Henri Poincaré called 'fruitful connections between unlinked elements'. And because I'm still searching for affinities, and in that search the imagination acts on the personal and truth becomes opaque and reality inchoate, and what really happened seventy years ago matters less than what *might* have happened, what could have happened. Does it really matter that my grandmother might never have met Yeats on an Athenry street, or that the remains inside that coffin that day might not have been his? Does it matter, when so much in our lives depends on chance, providence, on calamities that just miss us or demons that clip us?

My grandmother is long gone, her bones turned to dust. The three sons are gone too, and with them their memorized lines of Homer and Virgil. It is impossible now not to think of the nature of time, the journey of the soul, the image of Yeats poring over scripts at night and finding himself at some juncture, some interface between the human and spirit worlds, searching for signs and symbols to decipher Fate's plan, concocting his system of spirals and turning gyres to depict what he thought was the journey of a reincarnating soul.

He went on working to the very end. There's a photograph of him taken shortly before he died. He's sitting up in bed, frail, bearded, a scrawny white cat stretched out beside him. Even viewing it from this distance one feels like a trespasser, a voyeur at death's door. And yet he himself would not have flinched from such moments, but turned towards them, receptive, alert and – like Rilke – open to all realities, hidden and unhidden.

Gerard Smyth

NECESSARY CURSE

John Berryman's 'Dream Song 312', setting out the purpose of his 1960s
Dublin sojourn, is well-known for its opening declaration: 'I have moved
to Dublin to have it out with you, / majestic Shade'. But in the same
poem, Berryman admits that:

> For years then I forgot you, I put you down,
> ingratitude is the necessary curse
> of making things new ...

Well, for years after school I too cast him aside. Whether Yeats had been
a poet my schoolboy self had 'read so well' – as Berryman claimed he
once had – I am not sure. Certain poems were a staple of the old
curriculum of my schooldays: 'The Lake Isle', naturally – as well as 'The
Fisherman', 'The Wild Swans at Coole', 'The Song of Wandering Aengus',
'The Stolen Child'.

As sublime as these poems are, and instructive in the qualities that
lyric poetry must attain, it was a different Yeats to whom I later hearkened
and responded: the poet of late urgency, of passionate argumentative
speech. The daring Yeats spurred into song by 'lust and rage' seemed
more preferable to the one who gave us his wild swans and hazel wood,
the bee-loud glade and trysts down in the Salley Gardens.

Yes, for years I forgot him – and yet, his songs were always there in
the background, part of a national soundtrack. He gave us lines, phrases
and images that hit home in the way they expressed Ireland's spiritual,
material and political condition at particular moments – as a place
tarnished by its 'greasy till', that was 'no country for old men', where
'things fall apart' and where 'the centre cannot hold'. But above all his
electrifying 'terrible beauty' – still being born, still a work in progress.
Popular culture has become saturated in Yeatsian references, and the
danger with that is we may cease to hear the clarion notes.

When in the Sixties Berryman was noticing that the 'women of
Kilkenny weep when the team loses', the 'majestic Shade' had been dead
for twenty-eight years, yet many Irish poets were still manoeuvring
themselves from between the co-ordinates that he had laid down for Irish
poetry, learning how not to write in a Yeatsian mode. The exemplary
generation that faced that particular challenge, of *making things new* –
Thomas Kinsella, John Montague, Richard Murphy – had to discover
their own liberating examples in the wake of Yeats's forceful presence.
Photos of the poet as a young man show not only that *keep-your-distance*

glare, but also the gaze of a poet looking ahead at his own destiny. In his lifetime there were no games of one-upmanship; he doomed the reputations of his contemporaries, many of whom fooled themselves into thinking they were his kindred spirits (only that other Child of the Twilight, Austin Clarke, lived long enough to differentiate and transmute himself out of the Yeatsian mode and closer to the 'savage indignation' of the Swiftian breast). As for Kavanagh, he made 'the single, daring act of protest which pointed the way forward', as Eavan Boland has described the coming of the poet from Mucker.

So, is Yeats still traceable in the work of Irish poets, are today's poets still in dialogue with him? The dominant lyric strain in contemporary Irish poetry suggests that the infatuation with Yeats's music continues; that he resides in the inner ear of most Irish poets – if only as a song-maker whose cadences they must resist, whose legacy they must react against. His elevation of ordinary vernacular into artful expression still stands as an example to any young poet learning his or her trade. Perhaps what CK Williams had to say about Whitman's continuing influence on American poetry applies to Yeats in an Irish context: 'he defines for us the project of poetry, its possibilities, its parameters, in a way that's still in effect'.

What Yeats himself once had to say about his play *Cathleen ni Houlihan* (in *Explorations*) applies to the entire corpus of his work: the poems, plays and the prose writings: 'I had certain emotions about this country, and I gave those emotions expression for my own pleasure'. It was a slight understatement of course from the poet who set out to 'sweeten Ireland's wrong'. That enterprise involved the imagining and shaping of a nation – which he did through the radiance of his language and the single-minded intensity of thought wrapped in that language. It also involved playing a public role, which lifted him – and his poetry – to a position of national standing.

The poems of his I now most frequently turn to are not those of the 'sweet soul music' we heard in school, but the ones written in the midst of his 'old man's frenzy' towards the end: 'The Circus Animals' Desertion', 'Cuchulain Comforted', 'Under Ben Bulben', 'Beautiful Lofty Things', 'The Second Coming', 'Meditations in Time of Civil War', 'Sailing to Byzantium', and especially 'The Municipal Gallery Revisited'.

This last poem, Yeats's great litany of remembrance and summary of an age, was a return to a theme explored in the earlier 'In Memory of Major Robert Gregory', but here we have the old poet 'heart-smitten with emotions'. It is a magnificent reminder from a poet who appeared to stand in isolation and whose achievements were solitary ones, that in the end what matters is not necessarily 'the day's vanity, the night's remorse', but the friendships we forge in our lives, the countenances we are privileged to look upon.

WB Yeats

CRAZY JANE TALKS WITH THE BISHOP

I met the Bishop on the road
And much said he and I.
'Those breasts are flat and fallen now,
Those veins must soon be dry;
Live in a heavenly mansion,
Not in some foul sty.'

'Fair and foul are near of kin,
And fair needs foul,' I cried.
'My friends are gone, but that's a truth
Nor grave nor bed denied,
Learned in bodily lowliness
And in the heart's pride.

'A woman can be proud and stiff
When on love intent;
But Love has pitched his mansion in
The place of excrement;
For nothing can be sole or whole
That has not been rent.'

Sharon Olds

CRAZY SHARON TALKS TO THE BISHOP

I met the Bishop on the road
and much said he – same old porridge
I heard as a child, my little body
a 'foul sty.' And what did he mean,
'Love has pitched his mansion.' Maybe Love
pitched her silken tent – or was built
around it. Love has raised its dwelling
in the place of reproduction, which can be
fitted with an excellent device
which functions as a saving grace.
And maybe everything can be rent,
everything can be sole or whole – like an
asshole. I met a Bishop, once,
when I was a teenager mad as hell about
eternal fire and birth control,
we were sitting in my mother's living room,
I held out my fingers, and wiggled them at him,
and said 'I'm trying to make you levitate.'
He was not holding his crook, or his mitred
hat, but he was wearing a shirt
of magenta Egyptian cotton, woven and
dyed only for Bishops, and I said,
thinking myself quite the witty brat,
'That is the most beautiful shirt
I have ever seen, could you get me a shirt like that?'
Not seeing myself, the privilege
and ignorance of coming from a living room
like that. For I have built my poems in
the place of ignorant opulence.

WB Yeats

THE FOLLY OF BEING COMFORTED

One that is ever kind said yesterday:
'Your well-beloved's hair has threads of grey,
And little shadows come about her eyes;
Time can but make it easier to be wise
Though now it seems impossible, and so
All that you need is patience.'

                         Heart cries, 'No,
I have not a crumb of comfort, not a grain.
Time can but make her beauty over again:
Because of that great nobleness of hers
The fire that stirs about her, when she stirs,
Burns but more clearly. O she had not these ways
When all the wild summer was in her gaze.'

O heart! O heart! if she'd but turn her head,
You'd know the folly of being comforted.

Rita Ann Higgins

THE BOTTOM LASH

One that is ever kind said yesterday:
My dearest dear,
your temples are starting to resemble
the contents of our ash bucket
on a wet day.

What's with your eyelashes?
They grow more sparse by the tic tock.
Are you biting them off
or having them bitten off,
like the lovers do during intimacy
in the Trobriand islands?

You have no bottom lashes at all.
Personally, I wouldn't be seen out
without my bottom lash.
A bare bottom lash is tantamount
to social annihilation.

A word to the wise, my dearest dear,
the next time you lamp the hedger
you might ask him to clip clop
your inner and outer nostril hairs.
It's not a good look for a woman.

By the by, doteling,
I've noticed the veins on your neck
are bulging like billio
when a male of the species
walks into the room.
Is that a natural phenomenon
or is it a practised technique?
Up or down you'll get no accolades for it,
nor for the black pillows
under your balding eyes.
Apart from that, my dearest dear,
your beauty is second to none.

John Banville

MONUMENTS

WB Yeats, *The Tower* (Macmillan and Co, 1928).

WB Yeats's verse collection *The Tower,* which first appeared in February, 1928, is one of the greatest single volumes of poetry ever published – perhaps, indeed, the greatest. Among the twenty-one individual poems in the book, some of them written as far back as 1912, are a handful of transcendent masterpieces, such as 'Sailing to Byzantium', 'The Tower', 'Leda and the Swan', 'Among School Children', 'All Souls' Night', and those two twinned long poems, 'Meditations in Time of Civil War', and 'Nineteen Hundred and Nineteen', which deal with Ireland's misfortunes and murderous foolishnesses over the previous decade.

These poems are, to quote the poet himself, 'monuments of unaging intellect', but in the collection there is also a sprinkling of delightful, though dark, short pieces – 'Youth and Age', for instance:

> Much did I rage when young,
> Being by the world oppressed,
> But now with flattering tongue
> It speeds the parting guest.

The theme of old age and approaching death, wittily expressed in that little quatrain, permeates the collection. The poet was only sixty-two when the book was published, but the voice in the poems is that of an old man, raging against the body's betrayals and yearning rancorously after the power and pleasures of youth. For all the Celtic mist that drifts through and often obscures his early work, and the alchemical mumbo-jumbo of his highly personalized philosophy, if it may be called that, Yeats always had an acute, Nietzschean awareness of the body, of the fact that we are as much flesh as spirit; now, as he entered his sixties, the flesh, it seemed, was failing him.

In the years leading up to the publication of *The Tower* Yeats had been afflicted by a succession of debilitating illnesses. He suffered from high blood pressure and repeated bouts of influenza and congestion of the lungs; his sight was bad, and there were periods of mental depression. He had, in fact, little more than a decade of life remaining to him. His predicament infuriated and baffled him, but, as always, he turned his troubles into poetry, and in the process achieved a triumphant mastery of tone and content. These poems throb with a sense of physical immediacy matched, among the Modernists, perhaps only by Joyce and Picasso.

In the opening verses of the title poem, 'The Tower', we hear a new voice, irascible, lugubrious, impatient, self-mocking:

> What shall I do with this absurdity –
> O heart, O troubled heart – this caricature,
> Decrepit age that has been tied to me
> As to a dog's tail?

What is left to him now are but the things of the mind:

> It seems that I must bid the Muse go pack,
> Choose Plato and Plotinus for a friend
> Until imagination, ear and eye,
> Can be content with argument and deal
> In abstract things; or be derided by
> A sort of battered kettle at the heel.

Yet how can this be, the poet wonders, since:

> Never had I more
> Excited, passionate, fantastical
> Imagination, nor an ear and eye
> That more expected the impossible ...

In *Axel's Castle,* that extraordinarily shrewd and prescient study of contemporary writing and writers, published in 1931, the great American critic Edmund Wilson, speaking of *The Tower,* observed that in this work Yeats had passed into a new phase, 'in which he is closer to the common world than at any previous period ... He has become more plain-spoken, more humorous – his mind seems to run more frankly on his ordinary human satisfactions and chagrins: he is sometimes harsh, sometimes sensual, sometimes careless, sometimes coarse.'

And in a long, anonymous review in the *Times Literary Supplement,* the young Irish poet Austin Clarke found in these poems 'an imaginative and prosodic beauty that brings out the pure and impersonal joy of art'.

Clarke's formulation is particularly apt in relation to the first poem in the collection, the emblematic 'Sailing to Byzantium', the first of two superb works inspired by the Byzantine theme. Here the poet, succumbing to 'decrepit age', bids farewell to youthful fevers of the blood and summons the 'sages standing in God's holy fire' to be 'the singing masters of my soul', to consume his heart that is 'sick with desire /

And fastened to a dying animal' and gather him 'into the artifice of eternity':

> Once out of nature I shall never take
> My bodily form from any natural thing,
> But such a form as Grecian goldsmiths make
> Of hammered gold and gold enamelling
> To keep a drowsy emperor awake;
> Or set upon a golden bough to sing
> To lords and ladies of Byzantium
> Of what is past, or passing, or to come.

Of course, for all the poem's exquisite, jaded rhetoric, Yeats the poet had no intention whatever of resigning himself to a doddery old age. Indeed, he was to compose some of his most vigorous and compelling work in the years between the publication of *The Tower* and his death in the South of France in January 1939.

Great artists never let go to waste anything of experience, whether trivial or profound. Yeats used illness and the onset of age as the raw material out of which to make poetry. This had always been his method, in the fairy-infested work of his youth, in the mythologised loves of his early and middle years, and later on when, after living and working in London, he moved back to Dublin and transformed himself into the representative Irish poet of his time.

Along with his public commitments – his seat in the Irish Senate, the setting up, at the Abbey, of an Irish national theatre, and so much else – went an increasing fascination with the occult, culminating in that most peculiar prose work, *A Vision,* published in 1925, in which he forged a private mythology of supernatural signs and symbols. And 'forged', in all its fascinating ambiguousness, is surely the apt word here.

If for nothing else, *A Vision* is notable in that it includes the poem 'Leda and the Swan', so startling in its explicit erotic imagery, and ends with another magnificent poem, 'All Souls' Night', which the author set also at the close of *The Tower.* One is compelled to observe that, despite the inclusion of these two marvellous works, and some wonderful passages showing Yeats as a master of English prose, *A Vision* overall is the most awful tosh.

Once again, however, it provided him with 'metaphors for poetry', as he said. His indulgent but ever sensible wife, Georgie, had the measure of him in this regard. Writing to her friend, the poet Thomas MacGreevy, she wryly observed that in her husband's work 'All the pseudo-mystico-intellecto-nationalistico stuff ... isn't worth a trouser-button, or rather as a trouser-button is a most necessary article one might say a pillowcase button! As long as there was any gesture in it, as long as there was a war on and so on and so on, it was worth it'. Worth it, she means, in that it made for inspiration. 'There's nothing in his verse worth preserving,' Georgie added, 'but the personal'.

Yet Yeats was always torn between the personal and the public. In the opening verse of the poem 'Among School Children' he ruefully presents himself, in that famous formulation, as 'A sixty-year-old smiling public man', yet at the end we find him whirling in a sort of ecstatic dance, a dance in which art contemplates and interrogates itself and its effects –

> O body swayed to music, O brightening glance,
> How can we tell the dancer from the dance?

In the second half of his life Yeats the aesthete had indeed given way to the smiling, or more often indignantly scowling, public man. But even from his earliest years through to his late he had none of the aesthete's tendency to shrink from the common affairs of men, as he demonstrated for instance in his pugnacious commitment to the founding and maintaining of the Abbey Theatre – 'Players and painted stage took all my love', as he would write in that great poem, one of his last, 'The Circus Animals' Desertion' – and later, as the newly-founded Irish State blundered into civil war, he turned his energies, those he could spare from poetry, to the pursuit of politics.

He was a meddler of gigantic proportions. Of one of the many political shenanigans into which he sought to insert a spanner he wrote, with uncharacteristic candour: 'It was no business of mine, and that was precisely why I could not keep out of it.' From his place in the Senate, he thundered forth repeatedly on the issues of the day, glorying in his rhetorical powers and delighting in raising the hackles of those whom he saw as his enemies.

Particularly striking were his senatorial interventions in 1925 on the issue of divorce, when in his most famous speech he warned his fellow senators, and the wider Irish public, of the dangers of allowing the country to be made into a confessional state – 'once you attempt legislation on religious grounds you open the way for every kind of intolerance and for every kind of religious persecution,' he declared.

At the close of the speech, high of colour and sweating profusely, he soared to magnificent heights of eloquence, yet tarnished the overall effect with extravagant claims for the greatness of the Protestant Irish minority, who were 'no petty people ... one of the great stocks of Europe', he assured his awed and in many cases outraged listeners, a people who 'created most of the modern literature of this country' and 'created the best of its political intelligence'.

In his later life, Yeats's politics were, like the politics of so many of the intellectuals of his time, not pretty to contemplate. His unwavering contempt for democracy, which he saw as the triumph of shopkeepers and petty clerks over the nobility and the noble peasantry, and his detestation of socialism, what he called in his prose work *Autobiographies*, 'that mechanical eighteenth-century dream', hardened into a vision of imminent apocalypse out of which would come that infamous rough beast slouching towards Bethlehem to be born.

However, the poems in *The Tower*, despite an overall preoccupation with the political and social life of his time and place, sound a personal, almost a colloquial, note. Again and again the poet takes up the pose of the craggy curmudgeon, shaking his fist at the world and its idiocies, who yet is at moments capable of a flinty, self-deflating humour.

It is one of the smaller but still significant of modern Ireland's misfortunes that Yeats's politics, expressed most strongly through a shrill insistence on the superiority of his own caste, should have blunted the challenge he offered to the nation of living up to the noble image of it that he had wrought through his poetry, through the foundation of a National Theatre, and through his stance as a heroic public figure in a long line of Anglo-Irish intellectuals that included Edmund Burke, Bishop Berkeley and Jonathan Swift.

What he feared most, and most strongly warned against, in the late poems and his Senate speeches, was the rise to power in the nascent Irish state of the bourgeoisie, the fumblers in the greasy till, who would trample upon the 'many ingenious lovely things' that he wrote of in the poem 'Nineteen Hundred and Nineteen', those 'monuments of unaging intellect' that he and Lady Gregory and JM Synge, among a few privileged and privileging others, had laboured to create. Woe betide the land that needs heroes, Brecht drily observed, but perhaps worse woe betides the land that has a hero and refuses to heed him.

Chris Russell
Crazy Jane

Pen and Ink

Chris Russell
The Double Vision of Michael Robartes

Pen and Ink

Chris Russell
The Dying Lady

Pen and Ink

Chris Russell
The Fisherman

Pen and Ink

Responsibilities, by W. B. Yeats. The Cuala Press, Church-
town, Dundrum.

I live, so far as possible, among that more intelligently
active segment of the race which is concerned with today
and tomorrow; and, in consequence of this, whenever I mention Mr. Yeats I am apt to be assailed with questions: "Will
Mr. Yeats do anything more?", "Is Yeats in the movement?",
"How *can* the chap go on writing this sort of thing?"

And to these inquiries I can only say that Mr. Yeats'
vitality is quite unimpaired, and that I dare say he'll do a
good deal; and that up to date no one has shown any disposi-
tion to supersede him as the best poet in England, or any
likelihood of doing so for some time; and that after all Mr.
Yeats has brought a new music upon the harp, and that one
man seldom leads two movements to triumph, and that it is
quite enough that he should have brought in the sound of
keening and the skirl of the Irish ballads, and driven out
the sentimental cadence with memories of *The County of
Mayo* and *The Coolun;* and that the production of good
poetry is a very slow matter, and that, as touching the greatest
of dead poets, many of them could easily have left that
magnam partem, which keeps them with us, upon a single
quire of foolscap or at most upon two; and that there is no
need for a poet to repair each morning of his life to the
Piazza dei Signori to turn a new sort of somersault; and
that Mr. Yeats is so assuredly an immortal that there is no
need for him to recast his style to suit our winds of doctrine;
and that, all these things being so, there is nevertheless
a manifestly new note in his later work that they might do
worse than attend to.

"Is Mr. Yeats an Imagiste?" No, Mr. Yeats is a
symbolist, but he has written *des Images* as have many good
poets before him; so that is nothing against him, and he has
nothing against them (*les Imagistes*), at least so far as I
know—except what he calls "their devil's metres."

He has written *des Images* in such poems as *Braseal and*

the Fisherman; beginning, "Though you hide in the ebb and flow of the pale tide when the moon has set;" and he has driven out the inversion and written with prose directness in such lyrics as, "I heard the old men say everything alters"; and these things are not subject to a changing of the fashions. What I mean by the new note—you could hardly call it a change of style—was apparent four years ago in his *No Second Troy,* beginning, "Why should I blame her," and ending—

> Beauty like a tightened bow, a kind
> That is not natural in any age like this,
> Being high and solitary and most stern?
> Why, what could she have done being what she is?
> Was there another Troy for her to burn?

I am not sure that it becomes apparent in partial quotation, but with the appearance of *The Green Helmet and Other Poems* one felt that the minor note—I use the word strictly in the musical sense—had gone or was going out of his poetry; that he was at such a cross roads as we find in

> *Voi che intendendo il terzo ciel movete.*

And since that time one has felt his work becoming gaunter, seeking greater hardness of outline. I do not say that this is demonstrable by any particular passage. *Romantic Ireland's Dead and Gone* is no better than Red Hanrahan's song about Ireland, but it is harder. Mr. Yeats appears to have seen with the outer eye in *To a Child Dancing on the Shore* (the first poem, not the one printed in this issue). The hardness can perhaps be more easily noted in *The Magi.*

Such poems as *When Helen Lived* and *The Realists* serve at least to show that the tongue has not lost its cunning. On the other hand, it is impossible to take any interest in a poem like *The Two Kings*—one might as well read the *Idyls* of another. *The Grey Rock* is, I admit, obscure, but it outweighs this by a curious nobility, a nobility which is, to me at least, the very core of Mr. Yeats' production, the constant element of his writing.

In support of my prediction, or of my theories, regarding his change of manner, real or intended, we have at least two pronouncements of the poet himself, the first in *A Coat,** and the second, less formal, in the speech made at the Blunt presentation.† The verses, *A Coat,* should satisfy those who have complained of Mr. Yeats' four and forty followers, that they would "rather read their Yeats in the original." Mr. Yeats had indicated the feeling once before with

Tell me, do the wolf-dogs praise their fleas?

which is direct enough in all conscience, and free of the "glamour." I've not a word against the glamour as it appears in Yeats' early poems, but we have had so many other pseudo-glamours and glamourlets and mists and fogs since the nineties that one is about ready for hard light.

And this quality of hard light is precisely what one finds in the beginning of his *The Magi*:

Now as at all times I can see in the mind's eye,
In their stiff, painted clothes, the pale unsatisfied ones
Appear and disappear in the blue depth of the sky
With all their ancient faces like rain-beaten stones,
And all their helms of silver hovering side by side.

Of course a passage like that, a passage of *imagisme,* may occur in a poem not otherwise *imagiste,* in the same way that a lyrical passage may occur in a narrative, or in some poem not otherwise lyrical. There have always been two sorts of poetry which are, for me at least, the most "poetic;" they are firstly, the sort of poetry which seems to be music just forcing itself into articulate speech, and, secondly, that sort of poetry which seems as if sculpture or painting were just forced or forcing itself into words. The gulf between evocation and description, in this latter case, is the unbridgeable difference between genius and talent. It is perhaps the highest function of art that it should fill the mind with a noble profusion of sounds and images, that it should furnish the life of the mind with such accompaniment and surrounding. At any rate Mr. Yeats' work has done this in

* *Vide* this issue, page 60.
† *Vide* POETRY for March, 1914, p. 223.

the past and still continues to do so. The present volume contains the new metrical version of *The Hour Glass, The Grey Rock, The Two Kings,* and over thirty new lyrics, some of which have appeared in these pages, or appear in this issue. In the poems on the Irish gallery we find this author certainly at *prise* with things as they are and no longer romantically Celtic, so that a lot of his admirers will be rather displeased with the book. That is always a gain for a poet, for his admirers nearly always want him to "stay put," and they resent any signs of stirring, of new curiosity or of intellectual uneasiness. I have said the *The Grey Rock* was obscure; perhaps I should not have said so, but I think it demands unusually close attention. It is as obscure, at least, as *Sordello,* but I can not close without registering my admiration for it all the same.   *Ezra Pound.*

Stephen Lawlor
WBY (2015)
Monotype, paper size: 30H x 25W cm.

Martin Gale
Down by the Salley Gardens (2015)
Etching, edition of 40, paper size: 45H x 55W cm.

Michael Canning
1893 (2015)
Etching, edition of 40, paper size: 55H x 45W cm.

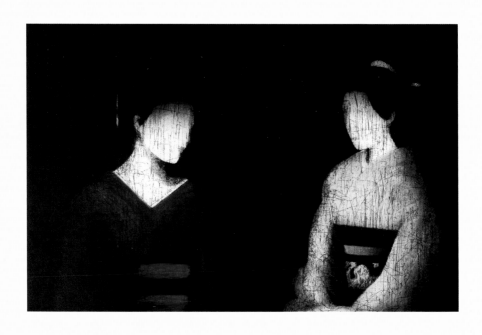

Stephen Lawlor
In Memory (2015)
Etching, edition of 40, paper size: 45H x 55W cm.

WBY, *Down by the Salley Gardens, 1893* and *In Memory* all feature in 'A lonely impulse of delight', an exhibition of visual art and the written word inspired by the poetry of WB Yeats. Other participants include **Norman Ackroyd**, **John Banville**, **Eavan Boland**, **Diana Copperwhite**, **Paul Muldoon**, **Edna O'Brien**, **Hughie O'Donoghue**, **Amelia Stein**, **Donald Teskey**, and **Colm Tóibín**.

'A lonely impulse of delight' runs from 27 November 2015 – 31 January 2016 at the SO Fine Art Editions Gallery, 10 South Anne St, Dublin 2.

www.sofinearteditions.com / **info@sofinearteditions**
087 2549884 / (01) 4721050

Fintan O'Toole

THE TIGHTENED BOW

I was thirteen or fourteen when I first read William Butler Yeats's poem about Maud Gonne, 'No Second Troy', and encountered its great line about her 'beauty like a tightened bow'. But I didn't at first understand that image. I thought he meant bow in the sense of a pretty ribbon in a girl's hair or, worse, tied around a box of chocolates. Even at that age this seemed a particularly banal image, frivolous and sugary sweet. And it did not seem to chime with the way the poem went on to talk about her beauty being 'high and solitary and most stern'. I had to re-read 'No Second Troy' a few times before it dawned on me that of course the tightened bow was not a girly ribbon. It was a bowstring drawn back to its fullest extent by an archer, the arrow poised across the frame, a dangerous, even deadly thing, caught in the moment of quivering stillness just before it is unleashed. The shock of the line then hit me like that arrow – the idea that beauty may not be pretty at all, that it could be perilous and frightening. But also the idea that the beautiful in art may not be a thing or an idea that has been fully achieved. It may be a moment of pure tension, a kind of arrested hovering between contradictory states. When I read Yeats, I find that what he delivers is not some kind of resolved poetic tranquillity. It is the creation of spaces where everything is pulled back as far as it can go and held there forever, ready for the release that it will always be refused.

In many ways I don't like Yeats. I don't like his snobbery, the contempt for ordinary urban life that runs through his work like a seam of sourness. I don't like the sexism of his repeated portrayal of women who became political activists as dried up old crones who have destroyed their lives by stepping outside their proper spheres. I don't like his preposterous portrayal of the Irish landed Protestant gentry as a heroic class. I don't like his authoritarian hauteur, his flirtation with fascism, his adoption of eugenics. In rejecting for the Abbey Theatre Sean O'Casey's play *The Silver Tassie*, Yeats accused O'Casey of writing out of his opinions, but of course Yeats writes out of his own opinions too and those opinions are sometimes creepy and obnoxious.

But actually not liking Yeats is, for me, a prerequisite for loving him. If I find myself nodding along in approval as I read a Yeats poem, which is not very often, I am probably experiencing it only in the single, rather flat dimension of its outward arguments. What I go to Yeats for is the tension. I have to read him against the grain of his opinions, and this keeps me in the right state of flux, drawn all the time between unease and delight, the urge to resist and the need to go with the flow. The bow stays tight.

Or, to use the image from one of my favourite plays, *At the Hawk's Well*, there is a tantalising awareness that the dusty stones of the well, the everyday limitations of Yeats's opinions, are wet with the sheen of something marvellous that has bubbled up from nowhere and left its trace. What I'm looking at with the literal eye is often crude stuff, heavy with the weight of historical prejudices, but what I become more conscious of is the evanescent, mysterious vestige of a transformative moment that has been and gone and that has passed out of time and history.

And this, for someone who deals in opinions as I do, is a blessing. As a young man with very strong and definite views about the world, I always found Yeats a bracing disturbance. I had to figure out what it was that drew me to him. At first, I was content to think that I loved him in spite of his outward opinions. Slowly, it dawned on me that this was not true: what is miraculous in his poems is precisely that what he so often transmutes into wonder, is trash. You can't have the first without the second. Without the foul rag and bone shop, there is no transcendence. The poems open up a space where everything holds everything else in check, where nothing is still or single, no thought is purely itself. Yeats forces me to engage with contradictions – his and my own.

The old bones of bad ideas and pompous prejudices peek through the beautiful flesh of Yeats's poems. The old rags of snobbery and bitterness leave their musty smell on his lyric grace. If they did not, there would not be the electric friction, the sense of something dangerous being held in check through a mighty effort of art and will. Others made art from their better selves; Yeats makes it from his whole self, including, crucially, the dislikable parts. If Yeats were, for me, more likable, his work would be tied up in neat bows of beauty. Because he sometimes repels, he binds me to those moments of contradiction that he turns into a pure and exhilarating tension.

Diarmaid Ferriter

THE HISTORY OF HIS TIME

On hearing that WB Yeats had been awarded the Nobel Prize for Literature in November 1923, WT Cosgrave, the President of the Executive Council of the Irish Free State, promptly congratulated him. Yeats replied that he thought the award was given to him not just for his own work, but was 'a part of Europe's welcome to the Free State, and I am very happy that it should be so'. It was a generous reply and indicated how comfortable Yeats was being identified with the new political establishment in Ireland in the early 1920s. A year previously, he had accepted with enthusiasm an invitation to become an Irish senator. Earlier in 1923 he had paid tribute to Arthur Griffith, one of the founders of the Free State, who had brought nobility to Irish politics he said, because he gave his faith 'not to an abstract theory, but to a conception of this historical nation – and we are all theory mad'.

A conception of the historical nation had been central to the cultural crusade of Yeats for many years and had ensured he was not always as comfortable with the establishment as he appeared after the Civil War. He lived through tumultuous political times and for me, as a historian of that era, his work offers powerful commentary, images and reflections on what the revolution meant as it was happening and how its legacy might play out. Although he often refuted the idea that he was any kind of politician, the drama of it all often exhilarated and frightened him and certainly provided stimulation for some of his most revered work, including one of the best-known poems in the English language: 'Easter 1916'.

The life-span of Yeats, 1865-1939, covered many of the most turbulent events of nineteenth- and twentieth-century Irish politics and culture, including the Celtic revival, Fenianism, home rule, the rise of Sinn Féin, the War of Independence and dramatic changes in Anglo-Irish relations. As pointed out by his biographer Roy Foster, Yeats had an acute sense of knowing how things would appear to people after the event, and 'His best-known poetry defines for many people the Irish identity which was forged in revolution ... his own discovery of his voice is often neatly paralleled with his country's discovery of independence'.

But his attitude to revolution in Ireland was complicated by the intersections and traditions of his own life, including important historical allegiances, personal relationships, and his ancient sense of divided identity which witnessed him dividing his time between England and Ireland, most notably during the War of Independence, when he paid only one visit to Ireland.

Before that, his love for Maud Gonne and his introduction to veteran Fenian John O'Leary led to him moving in Republican circles, but he grew tired of what he regarded as the pieties, hypocrisies and snobberies of the Catholic middle-class, most memorably in the poem 'September 1913', written to commemorate the date when Dublin Corporation rejected the proposed Hugh Lane Art Gallery:

> What need you, being come to sense,
> But fumble in a greasy till
> And add the halfpence to the pence
> And prayer to shivering prayer, until
> You have dried the marrow from the bone;
> For men were born to pray and save:
> Romantic Ireland's dead and gone,
> It's with O'Leary in the grave.

This was also Yeats as public commentator, and a man keen to fan the flames of controversy. The 1916 Rising forced him to revise this kind of satire, and indeed, his disillusionment with Irish nationalism. The Rising, and the events of the War of Independence and Civil War, forced him to reconsider the place of violence in personal and political renewal. 'Easter 1916' remains one of his best-known poems and it was an honest playing out of the doubts in his own mind about the wisdom of what had been done and the heroic bravery of the rebels. It is also a meditation on an idea borrowed from Maud Gonne – that tragic dignity had returned to Ireland. It enabled Yeats to place himself back into Irish history, rather than being an observer from the margins:

> I write it out in a verse –
> MacDonagh and MacBride
> And Connolly and Pearse
> Now and in time to be,
> Wherever green is worn,
> Are changed, changed utterly:
> A terrible beauty is born.

Dislocation was another frequent theme of his career, and this sense of removal caused tension between Yeats and his close friend Lady Gregory during the War of Independence. Lady Gregory was irritated when Yeats complained that 'the constant bad news from Ireland kills my power of poetical work'. From the safety and comfort of Oxford he penned the poem 'Reprisals', where he invoked the dignified death of Lady Gregory's son, Robert, who was killed as a British air force pilot during the war, to contrast it with the actions of the Black and Tans in Kiltartan, Co Galway, where Lady Gregory resided:

> Flit to Kiltartan cross and stay
> Till certain second thoughts have come
> Upon the cause you served, that we
> Imagined such a fine affair:
> Half-drunk or whole-mad soldiery
> Are murdering your tenants there.

Lady Gregory thought the poem was dishonest and would not let Yeats publish it. As recounted by Colm Tóibín, she recorded privately: 'Yeats only knows by hearsay while our troubles go on'. Gregory and Yeats also had different attitudes to the Republicans during the Civil War. Yeats sided firmly with the pro-Treaty side, and Gregory was more sympathetic to the Republicans, but their personal relationship weathered the storm. The murder in 1927 of Minister for Justice Kevin O'Higgins, who was a friend of Yeats, affected him deeply; indeed he drew parallels between O'Higgins's death and the fall of Parnell in the poem 'Parnell's Funeral':

> Had Cosgrave eaten Parnell's heart, the land's
> Imagination had been satisfied,
> Or lacking that, government in such hands,
> O'Higgins its sole statesman had not died.

During the 1920s Yeats grew disillusioned with the Free State, and it seemed with democracy itself. He maintained in his last speech to the Senate in 1928 that 'it is more desirable and more important to have able men in this House than to get representative men into this House', words that foreshadowed his future fling with extreme right-wing politics in the 1930s. The Irish revolution may have been over, but the poet's own political voyage was not yet complete.

His role in and response to the revolutionary era and its legacy generated an artistic output that I find irresistible as an historian of that period; it adds a depth and humanity to historical analysis that is unrivalled. TS Eliot eloquently identified the reason for this, shortly after Yeats's death: he described him as 'one of those few whose history is the history of their own time, who are part of the consciousness of an age which cannot be understood without them'.

Gerald Dawe

HIS FANATIC HEART

WB Yeats, *The Winding Stair and Other Poems* (Macmillan and Co, 1933).

Mr Yeats's new collection is a substantial volume of sixty-four poems and, including notes, amounts to one hundred pages. Considered as a companion volume to *The Tower* (1928), *The Winding Stair* demonstrates just how productive Mr Yeats, in his mid-to-late sixties, has become in a career that stretches back some five decades. This prolific output of poetry, drama, literary journalism, letters, memoirs, numerous editions of anthologies and his travels between these islands and further afield, are clear evidence of a life devoted to writing and exploring the historical and mystical world that we find ourselves in as clouds continue to darken on the political horizons of neighbouring European countries.

WB Yeats, long identified as Ireland's finest poet and internationally acknowledged as such with the awarding of the prestigious Nobel Prize for Literature in 1923, has produced a splendid, complicated, contradictory volume of poems in *The Winding Stair*, for the reason that the collection reads as if there are two distinct 'parts' with the latter responding and challenging the former. The development of image and theme which runs from the wonderful elegiac opening poem dedicated to Yeats's early friends, Eva Gore-Booth and her sister, Con, proceeds through various explorations and discoveries towards the tender landscape poem, 'Stream and Sun at Glendalough', a famous holy place in the annals of Irish spiritual history and enchantment. At which point *The Winding Stair* turns into the utterly different environment of *Words for Music Perhaps* (previously collected and published by the excellent Cuala Press in 1932), and concludes with a further sequence of eleven poems, 'A Woman Young and Old' which has formed part of the American edition of *The Winding Stair*, published in 1929.

These two sequences form an extraordinary bulkhead against the fading of creative energies which one gathers Mr Yeats had feared for himself during a long illness, as he recalls in the brief prefatory note to the illustrator, Edmund Dulac, the dedicatee of *The Winding Stair*:

> Then in the spring of 1929 life returned as an impression of the uncontrollable energy and daring of the great creators; it seemed that but for journalism and criticism, all that evasion and explanation, the world would be torn in pieces. I wrote 'Mad as the Mist and Snow', a mechanical little song, and after that almost all that group of poems called in memory of those exultant weeks 'Words for Music Perhaps'.

The energy and ebullient rhythms of the 'Crazy Jane' section of *Words for Music Perhaps* will last long in the reader's mind when some of the deeply rhetorical devices of Mr Yeats's stylish yet habitually enigmatic 'visionary' poems prove less amenable to the general reader. One thinks of elements of 'Vacillation', 'Byzantium', 'The Seven Sages', among others, where Yeats is examining both his own conscience and searching for his cultural and social roots in different times and places to the here and now. Echoing, perhaps, the poetry and drama of his late friend, John Millington Synge, the latter half of *The Winding Stair* amounts to a powerful poetic address all by itself.

But for this reader it is in those poems of a more defined landscape, with understandable characters at their centre, that Yeats produces a lyrical poise and imaginative pitch second to none. These are the poems one suspects he will be known by in the decades to come in his own country but also throughout the English-speaking world. Poems that mesh the history of Yeats's Ireland, and its struggle for self-determination and self-consciousness, with his own desire to see how his life and the lives of his friends are subject enough for great art.

Among these poems one can name 'In Memory of Eva Gore-Booth and Con Markiewicz', 'A Dialogue of Self and Soul' with its stunning last two lines ('We are blest by everything, / Everything we look upon is blest'), the magnificent 'Blood and the Moon', 'Coole Park, 1929' and the impeccable 'Coole and Ballylee, 1931'. The presence of ten short poems, often quatrains, provides the book with breathing spaces, pauses for thought. The poet might have reconsidered the wisdom of inserting dates to append to some poems but not others, while the note to 'Remorse for Intemperate Speech' distracts as much as it perplexes. To the refrain of each of its three five-line stanzas which refer to a 'fanatic' heart, Yeats inserts the following: 'I pronounce "fanatic" in what is, I suppose, the older and more Irish way, so that the last line of each stanza contains but two beats'. One can try it out:

> I ranted to the knave and fool,
> But outgrew that school,
> Would transform the part,
> Fit audience found, but cannot rule
> My fanatic heart.

Remorse and loss might underscore *The Winding Stair* but there is also an impressive authority of self-belief; an unbowing recognition of what has been achieved against the odds. It would be unwise to condemn outright Mr Yeats for some of his misguided alliances of late, a fault that travels across his generation (born in the latter stages of the nineteenth century, we should not forget) as they grapple with the unfolding events in Europe with barely concealed bewilderment. Indeed from the very beginning of *The Winding Stair* a sense of taking account sits passionately alongside the darkening feelings of disorder:

> Arise and bid me strike a match
> And strike another till time catch;
> Should the conflagration climb,
> Run till all the sages know.
> We the great gazebo built,
> They convicted us of guilt;
> Bid me strike a match and blow.

Who 'they' are is unanswered but in a book of many questions, the dominant sound is of a man interrogating his own past and what he set out to do for himself and make of the world he knew and/or inherited. Images of delicate timelessness are set against shocking images of suffering, literally page by page, as Yeats shapes the aesthetic narrative of his book, patterns which he works into the inner core of soundings, echoes, cross references, answering one poem with another, as in 'Blood and the Moon':

> Upon the dusty, glittering windows cling,
> And seem to cling upon the moonlit skies,
> Tortoiseshell butterflies, peacock butterflies,
> A couple of night-moths are on the wing.
> Is every modern nation like the tower,
> Half-dead at the top? No matter what I said,
> For wisdom is the property of the dead ...

To which sentiment in the facing six-line poem, 'Oil and Blood' death and its cerements are strangely present in the opening three lines:

> In tombs of gold and lapis lazuli
> Bodies of holy men and women exude
> Miraculous oil, odour of violet.

The Winding Stair and Other Poems treats of the great themes of mortality, love, regret, and sexuality with confidence and artistry yet at the book's epicentre, Mr Yeats is, as he reminds us in the prefacing note, dealing with deeply personal memories:

> I think I was roused to write 'Death' and 'Blood and the Moon' by the
> assassination of Kevin O'Higgins, the finest intellect in Irish public life,
> and, I think I may add, to some extent, my friend.

It will be recalled that Kevin O'Higgins was thirty-five years old when, as
Minister for Justice in the then fledging Irish Free State cabinet, he was
assassinated in south county Dublin in July 1927. *The Winding Stair*
however is not a poetry of confessions, but in its orchestration of image
and mood and in the enviable imitation of the great popular lyrical traditions of Irish ballad and song, Mr Yeats has fashioned a 'miraculous'
poetry of redemption and recovery, as he gathers the forces within him,
similar to that epiphanic moment he recalls in 'Vacillation', as a fifty year
old, alone 'in a crowded London shop':

> While on the shop and street I gazed
> My body of a sudden blazed;
> And twenty minutes more or less
> It seemed, so great my happiness,
> That I was blessed and could bless.

WB Yeats

When have I last looked on
The round green eyes and the long wavering bodies
Of the dark leopards of the moon?
All the wild witches, those most noble ladies,
For all their broom-sticks and their tears,
Their angry tears, are gone.
The holy centaurs of the hills are vanished;
I have nothing but the embittered sun;
Banished heroic mother moon and vanished,
And now that I have come to fifty years
I must endure the timid sun.

Kerry Hardie

LINES WRITTEN IN DEJECTION

When have I last looked on
a road I swerved across to miss a straying hen,
its verge not round-up'd, re-sown, planted, mown –
no float of cow-parsley or linnet's wings;
a river where they'd let me light a fire
or cook a fish without a permit for a hazel rod;
a child who'd take a boiled sweet from an ageing man;
an ageing man who'd hand a child a sweet;
wild bees not wiped out by varroa mite;
a leopard of the moon, a bee-loud glade.
And now that I have come to sixty years,
I must endure the buzz and bleep of phones.

WB Yeats

from A WOMAN YOUNG AND OLD

VI. CHOSEN

The lot of love is chosen. I learnt that much
Struggling for an image on the track
Of the whirling Zodiac.
Scarce did he my body touch,
Scarce sank he from the west
Or found a subterranean rest
On the maternal midnight of my breast
Before I had marked him on his northern way,
And seemed to stand although in bed I lay.

I struggled with the horror of daybreak,
I chose it for my lot! If questioned on
My utmost pleasure with a man
By some new-married bride, I take
That stillness for a theme
Where his heart my heart did seem
And both adrift on the miraculous stream
Where – wrote a learned astrologer –
The Zodiac is changed into a sphere.

Molly Peacock

I LEARNT THAT MUCH

The lot of love is chosen,
Then one of you gets sick –
The freely given frozen.
The look of love was chosen
Till illness's implosion:
Gone, the crooked face you picked.
It's just that one of you got sick.
The knot of love's not chosen.

Note

When I conducted a casual survey of North American poets about fifteen years ago for a book called *How to Read a Poem and Start a Poetry Circle*, I asked several dozen poets to name a single talismanic poem that influenced them. Though the poems were all different, the name of the poet who wrote more of those influential poems than all the others was WB Yeats. A surprising variety of poets, female and male, traditional to avant-garde, found unlocking sources for their own poems in Yeats's work. I'm no exception. As a poet who has the privilege of writing from the vantage of my age, I've reconnected to Yeats's poem 'A Woman Young and Old,' particularly to Part VI: 'Chosen.' I can't say I totally agree with the voice in the poem who says 'the lot of love is chosen'. It may be at first, but after a commitment, the lot of love is the rollercoaster you live on, and you cannot control the speed or curves. The initial attraction may feel chosen, but how a committed relationship plays out has much to do with the health of those two individuals. I believe this so wholeheartedly that I wrote a triolet-inspired response to just that part of the first line of the section. I tucked the second part of the line in as the title. Admittedly, this is a tiny response to a great literary figure. But little burrs from a large work can stick to a reader – and provoke passion in small packages.

Catriona Crowe

SAILING TO DRUMCLIFFE: THE REPATRIATION OF WB YEATS

There is not a great deal of material in the National Archives relating to WB Yeats – a letter of congratulations to him from WT Cosgrave on his receipt of the Nobel Prize, and a gracious reply, his original will and an accompanying schedule of assets, and a file dealing with inquiries from Belgium as to the State's plans for his centenary in 1965. Some of these documents can be seen on exhibition in the reading room lobby at the National Archives. As most people know, the great Yeats archive is to be found in the National Library, having been generously deposited there by his family.

But there are two files dealing with his death in 1939 and the repatriation of his remains in 1948 which illuminate the state's involvement with the end of his life and his subsequent repatriation nine years later. They are worth some description, containing as they do a number of letters from family and close friends, and details of the various plans and disputes which surrounded these events.

D/T S11135
WB YEATS: DEATH, 1939.

This file, from the Department of the Taoiseach, covers the period from Yeats's death in 1939 to 1965, the centenary of his birth. It consists largely of press cuttings, two from the *Irish Press* giving news of his death in Mentone on 28 January 1939, and an account of the attendance at the memorial service held for him in St Patrick's Cathedral on 6 February. Sympathy to the family was expressed by many, including James Joyce, Ezra Pound, John Masefield, Thomas MacGreevy, and practically all the old Abbey actors who had known him from his days with the Theatre. The German Minister, Herr Hempel, was the most senior foreign diplomat at the service. Six years later, then Taoiseach Eamon de Valera's courtesy call on him to sympathize on Hitler's death caused an international outcry.

Apart from a bill from Lennox Robinson, who was representing the government, for being driven from Glendalough House to the service (the bill was paid), most of the rest of the file consists of press cuttings relating to the return of Yeats's remains to Ireland, and the funeral at Drumcliffe in September 1948.

The file contains a letter from Jeanne Robert Foster, who (with financial assistance from the ever-generous John Quinn) had nursed and buried Yeats's father, John Butler Yeats, in New York in 1922. She requests the Irish Government to bring his body home and bury it next to his son's. The Government proclaimed this to be a matter for his relatives and declined any responsibility.

The last document on the file is a memorandum relating to the State's plans, if any, to mark the centenary of Yeats's birth in 1965. It concludes with the State's intention to issue a commemorative postage stamp, leaving any other events to the Summer School in Sligo. A stark contrast to the current plethora of activities relating to the 150th anniversary.

DFA 411/3/16/1R
RETURN TO IRELAND FROM FRANCE OF THE REMAINS OF MR WB YEATS.
Yeats had made it plain to his wife, George, that he wished to be buried in Drumcliffe, but he did not want a state funeral. She told Thomas MacGreevy: 'His actual words were, "If I die here bury me up there (at Roquebrune) and then in a year's time when the newspapers have forgotten me, dig me up and plant me in Sligo." He did not want the sort of funeral AE had.' The full story of the repatriation is told in the Epilogue to the second volume of Roy Foster's extraordinary biography, *WB Yeats – A Life, II: The Arch-Poet.* In brief, the plan had been to bring the body back to Ireland in September 1939, but the war intervened. In January 1948, Sligo Municipal Corporation raised the question of repatriation, and George set about making arrangements, only to find that the remains were not where they had been in 1939, having been moved within the cemetery. Identification to her satisfaction was carried out, and plans proceeded. (The recent discovery of contemporary French diplomatic documents seems to make it clear that the contents of the coffin are an assemblage of bones from the Roquebrune ossuary, hastily put together when repatriation was required. There is no guarantee, without DNA tests, that any of them are those of Yeats).

The file deals largely with the arrangements made by the Departments of External Affairs (Minister: Seán MacBride) and Defence (Minister: Thomas O'Higgins) to repatriate the body of WB Yeats from France to Ireland on the naval corvette *Macha.* The first document on the file, from 16 February 1948, lays out the itinerary of the corvette from Dublin to Villefranche, via Gibraltar, and back to Sligo, the voyage to commence on 25 August and to conclude on 17 September. There follows a letter from George Yeats to Seán MacBride dated 17 February:

Dear Seán,

You will have seen that the papers have got wind of the Corvette. Do let me know a date as soon as you can. I gather that Sligo is going to have a

general holiday on the day of WBY's arrival. Another tale is that the
County Council 'has tons of sand ready to go on the roads'. This piece
of information puzzles me. Why sand? WBY would have loved to know ...

Sand is usually put on roads when there is ice to be dealt with. Sligo,
even in 1948, was not likely to be suffering wintry conditions in
September. Perhaps the Council was preparing for every eventuality.

Villefranche turned out to be fully booked, so Nice was substituted as
the *Macha*'s port of call. Liam MacGowan, Features Editor of the *Irish
Press* ('Ireland's Greatest Newspaper'), writes to request permission to
travel on the corvette so that he can write a piece for the paper. He assures
the Secretary of the Department of External Affairs that he knows
accommodation will be limited, and he won't mind, as he is a seasoned
sailor. He is turned down.

The British Admiralty then instructs its outpost in Gibraltar to supply
the *Macha* with fuel and food ('small quantities of fresh meat and vegeta-
bles, including potatoes') on 30 August / 1 September, when it will be
docking there.

On 1 September, when the *Macha* is well underway, Lennox Robinson
writes to MacBride:

> Dear Seán,
>
> Just to confirm our conversation of yesterday; let me know in good time
> the arrangements about WBY. And I quite understand that your
> department cannot help in whatever travelling we do. I shall go anyway,
> even if I have to walk to Sligo ...

No payment for transport this time.

There are several documents dealing with the issue of whether the
corvette can berth at Sligo rather than the naval choice, Galway. Galway
was deemed to be safer, as Sligo harbour apparently was too shallow to
take the *Macha*. This was hotly disputed by various local dignitaries, one
of whom wrote to Lennox Robinson as follows:

> It is only right that WB Yeats should sail into Sligo Bay with Ben Bulben
> and Knocknarea on either side and Lissadell, Ballisodare and Sligo itself
> stretched out before him. – Why should he go to Galway? Sligo wants
> him – and always did – her harbour is quite deep enough to take the
> *Macha*. Please tell this to the organising body in Dublin. Sligo Harbour
> has been ignored for long enough – but this last blow has been too
> much – it is unbearable!

This letter is signed 'Jill', probably Jill Noone, a Sligo actress whom
Robinson had asked to reserve a room for him in the Grand Hotel.

Robinson forwarded this letter on to MacBride, noting 'Sligo is getting very indignant. The idea of that upstart Galway!!!' The authorities, however, remained adamant in their adherence to the upstart, and local indignation had to be quashed.

The government issued a press release on 13 September announcing the return of the body:

> The Government Information Bureau announce that the Corvette L.É. *Macha*, bearing the remains of the late WB Yeats, will dock at Galway at approximately 6 am on the morning of Friday, the 17th September. The coffin, containing the remains, will be transferred to a motor hearse at 7.30 am, and the cortège will leave for Sligo shortly afterwards.
>
> It will be met at the boundary of the Borough at about noon by the Mayor and members of Sligo Corporation and County Council, and will be escorted to Quay Street, where it will remain, outside the Town Hall, from approximately 12 noon until 2 pm. At 2 pm, the funeral will proceed to Drumcliffe where the final interment will take place.
>
> In deference to the expressed wishes of the poet's family, there will be no State ceremonial, with the exception of the provision of a Military Guard of Honour for the remains while they lie in Sligo.
>
> The Government was, of course, desirous to accord full State honours in connection with the funeral, but considered it proper to respect the wishes of the poet's relatives.
>
> Accordingly, all the arrangements in connection with the bringing home of the poet's remains have been carried out in accordance with the wishes of and in consultation with the Yeats family.

There were definite sour grapes about being denied a state funeral. The inter-party government, Ireland's first, could have done with a propaganda coup of that stature. However, they made the best of what they had, and gamely footed the bill for the repatriation.

Sean Murphy, the Irish Minister to France, was present at Roquebrune for the transfer of the coffin to the *Macha*. 'At Roquebrune the coffin was on two trestles on the village square surrounded by a small guard of honour who presented arms as the hearse moved off. The Mayor and local Council were present. One of the Councillors, who was also a doctor, made a short speech of adieu in which he described Yeats as the Irish Victor Hugo.' Murphy goes on to describe the arrival of the coffin in Nice, further guards of honour, a band, and many dignitaries. A later letter mentions 'certain expenses to settle with regard to the leaden coffin and the transport'. Although the French were clearly happy to assist in the repatriation, they weren't going to do it for nothing.

In the middle of the file there is a telegram (with an ad for the Irish Sweepstakes on the back) from John Hall Wheelock, an American poet and editor at Scribner, to Seán MacBride, reading 'Praise God for Yeats'. There is much polite correspondence thanking the French for their help at Roquebrune and Nice, and the British for their help at Gibraltar. Also a letter from MacBride to George forwarding to her documents relating to the French part of the journey, including the speech made by M. Otto, the doctor at Roquebrune, and a copy of the poem he recited.

There is a full account of the *Macha*'s voyage, recounting details of the crew's two days in Gibraltar, where they were treated to a cocktail party, a formal lunch, a formal dinner, an informal supper, a guided trip around the Rock and an 'entertainment' by Irish nurses at the local hospital. They also visited Archbishop Fitzgerald, from Midleton, Co Cork. They experienced high winds, torrential rain and 'vivid lightning' on their way to Nice. On their return journey, there were further high jinks at Gibraltar (Anglo-Irish relations appear to have been very cordial), and then set off without incident to Galway. The trip was adjudged 'a complete success', despite the crew being too hot in their dress uniforms ('murderous') and the radar packing in two days after departure.

Most of the rest of the file deals with the important matter of payments for the repatriation. There is a letter from our intrepid Minister in London, John Dulanty, stating that Harold MacMillan is 'having great difficulties in finding any copies' of Yeats's *Collected Poems* and *Collected Plays* (he was out of print at this time). MacBride writes to George in February 1949 thanking her for her 'great kindness in lending us the masks for the production of *At the Hawk's Well* which we presented here on the occasion of the Diplomatic Reception', and returning the masks to her. It appears that the navy shot some film of the ceremony at Roquebrune, in which a number of people express interest, but they are told it 'is the property of the Eastern Command Welfare Board' and costs of copying it would be prohibitive. One wonders where it is now. The last document on the file, dated 3 November 1949 requests payment of pilotage fees arising out of the *Macha*'s visit to Nice – £3. 4. 11.

These files provide an interesting glimpse into the state's involvement in one of the most important public events of the late 1940s, in which there was considerable interaction by the population and the press. We get material from George Yeats (mischievous and funny), from Seán MacBride (who of course knew Yeats well and was now presiding over his return to Ireland), from Sean Murphy, John Dulanty and Valentine Iremonger (all working for the Department of External Affairs), plus a detailed account of a unique voyage by one of our naval vessels, and reference to what sounds like an interesting film of the removal of the body. It is clear that the state would have loved an official funeral, but George stuck fast to her husband's wishes and got what she wanted. The dispute between Galway and Sligo as to where the remains should be landed reminds us that, as always, all politics are local.

Kevin Barry

FLOWERS IN HIS HAIR

It is the ninth of June and a springtime as chilling as evil has at last ended in Co Sligo. I leave the barracks and crawl into the light and shudder off the last of the cold spring and winter. I take out the bike and cycle around the dragonfly haunts of Lough Arrow. There are a few fishing boats out but the roads are almost empty and the drowsiness of summer is falling at last over the reed fields and the silvering water. I cut onto the road south from Corrigeenroe towards Boyle, and I coast now at a whirring height above the shore of Lough Key, our sisterly lake – it is just a few miles south of the barracks, and the treetops here are bunched and ferocious with the new growth. The green these past few days has emerged fully and as swiftly as though in time-lapse photography. I can see down to the small islands in the centre of the lake and, as always when I pass by here, I think – for just the fleetest moment, until the view passes with the whirring of the spokes – about William Butler Yeats.

In the early 1890s, he formulated a plan to buy one of the islands. He wished to set up on Castle Island a Celtic Mystical Order, or in other words a commune, a congregation of like-minded souls devoted to occultism, arcane practices, and to the sweet rotations of polyamorous love. Those were the sweetest days of his life, and those were the sweet nights, when he rolled naked by moonlight on the sands at Rosses, under the influence of tincture of cannabis – most civilly available, then, from the chemist shop in Sligo town – and there were voices in the wind, and there were voices on the waves that broke and laced on the shore, and Sligo bay spoke to him in its deep, tremorous voice.

He was born about a century too soon. Auden said once that he was essentially a southern Californian and I believe that is precisely what he was. He was drawn to the water and he was drawn to the light. He was of the third sex. He knew that there was another world beneath the drear surface of ours – he could tune into it at will. He was of an archetype that only became fully legible in the late 1960s or early 1970s – he was in all essentials a hippy-businessman type, or a stoner-entrepreneur. He had a wild tremendous energy. He should have been born in Redondo Beach in 1952. He would have worn flowers in his hair. He would have loved some psychedelic Sally with a painted face. I can see his arch-patrician brow now as it stares into the mystic surf. He was not meant for the grey skies; he was not meant for the drear. He sought to transform this place and he almost could have, and almost did. The commune never happened; plans changed.

Rays of occult sunlight burn across the treetops now as I retrace the road
and cycle my ritual route from Roscommon back into Co Sligo again.
Summer is here at last and in the near distance the Yeatsian coachloads
are choking up the N4 – he would have charged those goons high ticket
prices, he would have scalped the fuckers alive. He wanted free love; he
wanted water and light. The gothical ruin rises from Castle Island still
and it reaches for his sky. The south of France became his California by
default but it was decades too soon. He should have lived by the Pacific.
He should have felt each day the warm sunlight on his skin.

Joseph O'Connor

YEATS IS MY MOTHER

Yeats is my mother, the last time I saw her, quoting 'Easter 1916' at the rainfall of her life.

He's a Saturday morning lecture in UCD, in the bitterly cold winter of 1981, Gus Martin going through drafts of 'The Sorrow of Love' and pointing out that one phrase survives almost every redraft: 'A girl arose that had red mournful lips'.

'He knows when he's onto a good thing,' Gus says.

Yeats is a haughty stare on a banknote, the face of an exquisitely corrupt cardinal.

Yeats is the realizer that everything contains its opposite, that beauty can be terrible, that fire can be simple, that all things start in the foul rag and bone shop of the heart, that nothing can be whole that has not been rent, that beauty is a tightened bow.

Yeats is daft as a bag of spanners.

Theosophy. Ghosts. Automatic writing. Other muppetry.

Yeats is a committee man, a goer-to-meetings.

Yeats is an Irishman who was only in a pub once. (Toner's, Baggot Street, reportedly).

Yeats is a tower in Gort, a house in Merrion Square, a gentlemen's club in London, a Noh theatre in Japan, a conversation with Synge, whom he envied, in Paris. He's all these things, and none of them, and more.

(Synge writes: 'People like Yeats who sneer at old fashioned goodness and steadiness in women seem to want to rob the world of what is most sacred in it').

Two interesting anagrams can be made of 'William Butler Yeats':
1) A really sublime twit.
2) Wait, I'm really subtle.

Yeats is the gateway through which poetry first beckoned to hundreds of thousands of Irish schoolchildren, and we owe him so much, those of us who love poems, for the secret country of pleasures we found in there, with its canal banks of Kavanagh and its meadowlands of Seamus and its brooks trickling down from the slopes of Mount Muldoon and its lighthouses called Meehan and Durcan and Morrissey and its shining northern town, Carson City. There's no map of this homeland but anyone can go there, by flying to a place where Ryanair can't take you. Dorgan's boat plies the main, Fallon's Gallery is astounding, Nuala the *spéirbhean* spins beauty from dust. For multitudes who got healed there, Yeats was the first conduit. Our portal, our passport, our pillow.

Yeats is the *Soundings* anthology. He's a question on the Leaving.

Will Yeats come up?

Are you serious?

He's *always* coming up, and he always will. He came up a lot when he was alive – he made certain of that – and the relatively minor matter of Sligo-based burial (or Sligo-based *non*-burial!) is not going to be keeping him down.

This is a gentleman who wrote his own *tombstone*.

So, yes. He'll be coming up.

In David Mamet's play *Glengarry Glen Ross*, the salesmen are constantly being threatened by their sadistic boss that if they don't improve their numbers he'll go downtown and report them to the feared 'Mitch and Murray'.

That's how I feel about Yeats. Like someone's going to *inform* on me to him.

('Write another sentence as bad as that, I'm goin' downtown and see Yeats. Don't say I didn't warn your ass. Quit snivellin'!').

'Rime wilts all beauty' and 'ability matures well' are only two more of the available anagrams. But this must stop.

Yeats is 'Troy' by Sinéad O'Connor and 'The Stolen Child' by Mike Scott.

And he's somewhere in the background of Van Morrison's 'Madam George'. (Yeats was married to a George, perhaps that's it).

Yeats is my English teacher, with tears of frustration, saying 'Yeats is the greatest poet ever lived or ever will.' But I, being young and foolish, with her could not agree.

> Down by the Salley gardens, Mad Ireland walked with Yeats / and 'hurt' him into poetry / so Auden sadly states / And under bare Ben Bulben's head / Mad Ireland came to leech/while thieving his one-liners/for a politician's speech.

He's the wild swans at Coole.

He's the moorhen's call.

He's away with the fairies and he's scolding the audience.

You have disgraced yourselves again!

Sock it to 'em, Bill.

Pack of till-fumbling hypocrites.

(When you've been Yeatsed, you stay Yeatsed).

Yeats tommy-gunned Ireland with a hail of words that were true when he wrote them and, oddly, are truer today, perhaps.

> We had fed the heart on fantasies,
> The heart's grown brutal from the fare;
> More substance in our enmities
> Than in our love ...

He's Billy the Kid. Then he's William the Conqueror. He's YEATS, for God's sake.

What is he like?

If he hadn't existed, we'd have needed to invent him.

That's what we did, of course.

John Montague

LEADING THE DANCE

WB Yeats, *Words For Music Perhaps and Other Poems* (Cuala Press, 1932).

After the success of the 'Yes' campaign in Ireland's recent marriage equality referendum, *Words for Music Perhaps* makes an auspicious debut. When the Bishop admonishes Crazy Jane to 'Live in a heavenly mansion, / Not in some foul sty', her reply distils all of the rage, pride and love that propelled the 'Yes' campaign to victory. So she and Jack the Journeyman can disport in the hills while the little army of bishops huddles in its chill palaces, for 'The Bishop has a skin, God knows, / Wrinkled like the foot of a goose'.

It is remarkable how our colleague, Mr Yeats, an earnest, large-footed young gentleman from the other tradition, has managed to shamble into cottage kitchens, and absorb some of their language and their lore. Except, of course, that the Irish have a great talent for polite teasing, and some might have been indulging our bespectacled friend by telling him what he plainly wanted to hear.

Crazy Jane, it seems, is based on an old lady who lived in a cottage near Gort, a local wise woman called Cracked Mary, whose episodes of flamboyant drunkenness 'are of an epic magnificence'. (Though they seem mild to me, compared to the execrations of Padna Hyland at the toss pit in Abbylara, Co Longford, or the litany of curses from De Valera Dalton in the local hostelry).

In this volume, as in so many previous ones, Mr Yeats approaches the mystical through contrast and paradox. In 'Among School Children' he had already taught us that 'Labour is blossoming or dancing where / The body is not bruised to pleasure soul', and reminded us that 'Solider Aristotle played the taws / Upon the bottom of a king of kings'. And now we have Crazy Jane, declaring in her wisdom: 'Love has pitched his mansion in / The place of excrement'. Likewise, in 'Among School Children', the poet addressed the chestnut tree: 'Are you the leaf, the blossom or the bole?' If Mr Yeats is pondering the mysteries of the body, and of the spirit which is housed within it, if he is asking: *What is wholeness, and where does our essence lie?* then the answer is provided now by Crazy Jane: 'For nothing can be sole or whole / That has not been rent'. Wholeness or completion can only evolve from a tearing; we must separate in order to connect. This poet is not renowned for puns, but 'Crazy Jane talks with the Bishop' abounds with them: sole / soul and whole / hole are but two examples.

Despite the book's title, there are very few examples of Mr Yeats's poems being set to music (hence, perhaps, the *Perhaps* after *Words for Music*). René Char's *Le Marteau sans maître* was wrought into music by Pierre Boulez, and poems by Hesse served as settings for Strauss's *Last Songs*, but composers have not seized on Yeats in the same way. Despite his melodious verse he himself has no ear for music; in the famous BBC recording, he can be heard trying to sing, but it sounds more like cawing. And one has the impression that he actually does not know much about Irish music, either traditional or contemporary, even though Elvis Costello maintains he collaborated with the poet on 'A Drunken Man's Praise of Sobriety', which I have heard performed in the Abbey Theatre, where I also heard Paddy Moloney provide a musical background for 'The Dreaming of the Bones'.

So a central paradox of Yeats's career is that while he is tone-deaf, he is capable of great poetic music, perhaps the most sonorous since Tennyson. And he was a master of the raw ballad, maybe too much so, as Patrick Kavanagh (that Dr Johnson from Monaghan) seems to suggest when he accuses Mr Yeats's disciple, FR Higgins, and by implication Yeats himself, of stage-Irishry, or what PK derisively calls 'buck-lepping'. Yet the Muse, according to Yeats, prefers merry roguish lads. (There is a hilarious account of a totally drunken dinner at the Irish Academy of Letters where Higgins and Frank O'Connor sang *The Curse of Cromwell* while WB barred the door).

Mr Yeats is certainly concerned with Irishry and Irishness, and is haunted by the medieval Irish lyric: '"*I am of Ireland, / And the Holy Land of Ireland, / And time runs on*"'. But the poet seems to fear a growing discord in Ireland and elsewhere, for '"The fiddlers are all thumbs, / Or the fiddle-string accursed, / The drums and the kettledrums / And the trumpets are all burst"'.

For despite Crazy Jane's ancient entreaty, '"*Come out of charity / And dance with me in Ireland*"', he 'Had turned his stately head' admonishing her that '"the night grows rough"'. But the reader feels that this 'One solitary man / Of all that rambled there', this lyrical yet unmusical poet, this endearingly clumsy man who yet revered the dance, will continue to lead it, as he has done in these poems.

WB Yeats

HIGH TALK

Processions that lack high stilts have nothing that catches the eye.
What if my great-granddad had a pair that were twenty foot high,
And mine were but fifteen foot, no modern stalks upon higher,
Some rogue of the world stole them to patch up a fence or a fire.
Because piebald ponies, led bears, caged lions, make but poor shows,
Because children demand Daddy-long-legs upon his timber toes,
Because women in the upper stories demand a face at the pane
That patching old heels they may shriek, I take to chisel and plane.

Malachi Stilt-Jack am I, whatever I learned has run wild,
From collar to collar, from stilt to stilt, from father to child.
All metaphor, Malachi, stilts and all. A barnacle goose
Far up in the stretches of night; night splits and the dawn breaks loose;
I, through the terrible novelty of light, stalk on, stalk on;
Those great sea-horses bare their teeth and laugh at the dawn.

Sinéad Morrissey

AT THE MOSCOW STATE CIRCUS

Processions that lack high stilts have nothing that catches the eye
and yes, by three hours in, we're jaded, frankly. The baby
tiger, stupid with drugs, we fondled and got flashed with,
has been taken away by the scruff of his silver chain and the woman
undressing and dressing herself again inside a fire-filled hoop
without a single glimmer of skin is running out
of costumes. How this cacophonous *spectaculum* will finish
is anybody's guess; our kids are so bored and sugared up
they're about to froth with tears, like soda fountains.

                                        Mozart's 25th.
Acrobats in wigs in lace in Amadeus cuffs file into place
and we're staring once it starts. One by one they jackknife

onto a trampoline and using their dear launched breakable
selves as pens, as flares, sketch out for us in air what isn't there:
a simple X, then denser, higher – cat's-cradle architecture
strung taught as piano wire, rigging, fountains, the winged
horse in the sky, all his star-points joined together, and as
they angle backwards to land like so many stackable chairs
on their comrades' shoulders, it's not just the absence
of gravity we'll remember – bodies being impossible–
but the way we imagined we could reach out and touch
the co-ordinates for the Battle of Stalingrad.

WB Yeats

BYZANTIUM

The unpurged images of day recede;
The Emperor's drunken soldiery are abed;
Night resonance recedes, night-walkers' song
After great cathedral gong;
A starlit or a moonlit dome disdains
All that man is,
All mere complexities,
The fury and the mire of human veins.

Before me floats an image, man or shade,
Shade more than man, more image than a shade;
For Hades' bobbin bound in mummy-cloth
May unwind the winding path;
A mouth that has no moisture and no breath
Breathless mouths may summon;
I hail the superhuman;
I call it death-in-life and life-in-death.

Miracle, bird or golden handiwork,
More miracle than bird or handiwork,
Planted on the starlit golden bough,
Can like the cocks of Hades crow,
Or, by the moon embittered, scorn aloud
In glory of changeless metal
Common bird or petal
And all complexities of mire or blood.

At midnight on the Emperor's pavement flit
Flames that no faggot feeds, nor steel has lit,
Nor storm disturbs, flames begotten of flame,
Where blood-begotten spirits come
And all complexities of fury leave,
Dying into a dance,
An agony of trance,
An agony of flame that cannot singe a sleeve.

Astraddle on the dolphin's mire and blood,
Spirit after spirit! The smithies break the flood,
The golden smithies of the Emperor!
Marbles of the dancing floor
Break bitter furies of complexity,
Those images that yet
Fresh images beget,
That dolphin-torn, that gong-tormented sea.

James Harpur

The unpurged images of day recede.

We're all abed, a ghost train going nowhere.

A boy jerks up and moans, dream-violated.

The flashlight of the duty prefect's torch
drains blood from every face it hits;
     I hear
a sleeper's unhinged chuckle; feral snores.

I start to drift … before me float four shades
who tilt a bed up ninety odd degrees –
a boy-cum-mattress crumples to the floor
his piggy grunts converging to a cry
I panic-pray *dear god, not me, please, please*

an agony of trance … I sense them pass me by

returning to the dark from which they've crept

the corner of your sleep that's never slept.

Rowan Williams

PILGRIMAGE

The first poem by Yeats I read – at the not very competent age of around
ten, I think – was 'The Magi', in an anthology of poems about the three
wise men of the Christmas story. Describing it as a Christmas poem is a
bit like describing Wagner's *Ring* as a sword-and-sorcery fantasy. But
what struck an immediate chord, even at a tender age, was the
overwhelming sense of sombre but intense emotion caught in hieratic
form, tears of stone. A paradox, given that it's a poem about passionate
restlessness: the magi, all silver and stone, as still as playing cards ('stiff,
painted clothes'), represent the unchanging reality of desire, the eros
that seeks deeper immersion in something uncontrollable, violent, even,
something that will finally and decisively dissolve restlessness, not in rest
but in apocalyptic convulsion. The apparent 'turbulence' of Calvary
doesn't work: the mystery that matters is what is encrypted on the
'bestial floor', not a million miles, perhaps, from the 'foul rag and bone
shop of the heart', granted Geoffrey Hill's justifiably suspicious
comments on the over-neatness of that phrase. When, some years later, I
read 'The Second Coming' at school and the Byzantium poems, I think I
read them (even if I didn't have the words to describe it accurately at the
time) as embodying a poetics struggling to hold together something
beautiful and frighteningly anarchic in a verbal scheme that evoked and
sometimes enacted magical or ritual gesture. I was absorbing a sense that
poetry needed a proximity to but not an identification with this ritual
register if it were to manage the seriousness of disruption and public as
well as private chaos; that, as the Byzantium poems suggest, only a
highly-wrought 'post-humanist' perspective can speak a truth that is
more than local and trivial, even about local and trivial matters. But the
aesthetic is more complex than that: the still later poetry shows at the
same time a passionate search for aphoristic simplicity, the poetic self-
evidence of the folk-song, and their authority is caught up in this. Not
simply ritual or magic as such; but a verbal form in which there is the
kind of closure that both defies argument and generates new form
('fresh images beget').

Yeats is for a good many twentieth-century poets (from Auden to RS
Thomas) an inescapable interlocutor who at the same time cannot serve
as a model. He is surprisingly hard to parody (unlike most of the other
giants of the era). His impact on others is seldom if ever through
inducing others to echo his idioms, his metaphors or even his 'register'; it
is perhaps better seen as setting a model of the sort of closure just

mentioned. And Yeats's unending pursuit of this is, of course, what brings him back from what I've just called the post-humanist, the dismayed contemplation of the 'dying animal', to the various lusts and rages embodied in the poetry of the last years – the poetry that evidently so fascinated and troubled Eliot and helped to shape the 'familiar compound ghost' of 'Little Gidding' (not to mention the 'folly' of old men in 'East Coker'). Eliot passes a severe moral and spiritual judgement here; but there are other issues to weigh. In moving away from 'Byzantium', Yeats affirms a central poetic irony, that the eros for the consumingly beautiful and anarchic (and non-human) appears also as an eros for what is here and now – a homesick longing for the actuality of flesh in this moment. What I am divided from is not the eschatological vision of the magi or the icy filigree of Byzantium that holds the explosive codes of life, but the flesh that I in fact am. If poetry needs proximity to ritual, if it is in some important sense magical, it also needs the attempt at the fusion of word and sensual being. The bestial floor is here. The country for old men is not after all the Byzantine myth, but a place of fully named and embodied passion, even if this is a passion over loss or impotence: a place of anger and what Yeats famously calls 'gaiety' in one of the most arresting poems of the last years, 'Lapis Lazuli', 'Gaiety transfiguring all that dread', the gaiety of the tragic protagonist fully aware of utter waste.

Where Yeats finally arrives is a difficult place, a place in which, in one sense, nothing is 'reconciled': passion is acknowledged, unleashed, for all that this comes too late (as Crazy Jane might see it), because only in the speaking of the rage of unsatisfied eros do we speak what we actually are, so that our words have both authority and generativity. Yeats will neither deny nor assimilate or naturalize loss in these late writings. It is an appropriately 'pagan' aesthetic, more deeply and consistently so than anything in his mythologies; a late style with a vengeance. But its energy is – if one more paradox can be managed – not a protest, a resentment, but a bare articulating of the present as the place of loss – and, precisely in articulating this place, this here and now, a moment of almost intolerable celebration, gaiety, dread absorbed in the glittering eye. Not the only aesthetic of late style, nor of the poetic enterprise more generally, but one that can be seen growing out of the magian pilgrimage of dissatisfaction.

Donal Ryan

NIRVANA

When I was fourteen I wrote a letter to a girl I'd met on a holiday with my family in the west of Ireland. I included a poem I'd written for her, which I called 'Shy One'. The poem closely resembled Yeats's 'To an Isle in the Water'. In fact, the poem was, almost word for word, Yeats's 'To an Isle in the Water'. She wrote back, thanking me for the very nice poem, and explaining that, as she attended a boarding school and there was a distance of eighty miles between our homes, she didn't feel there was any point in 'carrying on our relationship'. I blamed Yeats for this crash and burn, specifically for the line 'She carries in the dishes'. He should have considered that such an image could some day erode the chances of a lovesick, plagiarising idiot. I soon forgave him, though.

Yeats sat somewhere very close to the eye of the maelstrom of cultural influences that swirled and seethed through my teenage mind. He and Kurt Cobain occupied the same plane in my consciousness, both artists floppy of fringe and famously angst-ridden. They seemed to me to be temporally un-synced brothers in heroic suffering: Kurt Cobain giving plaintive, wailing voice in his songs to the pain caused in his youth by 'that terrible divorce', and Yeats drawing on his unrequited love for Maud Gonne. I drew them both in charcoal, standing side by side. I copied my Yeats from the pencil drawing of him on the inside leaf of my *Collected Poems* and my Cobain from a drawing a more talented classmate had done. These third-hand renderings caused my father to declare me a genius and my mother to shake her head and wonder aloud what kind of fooling I'd been at inside in my room when I should have been studying.

I sold part of my record collection to buy certain contraband and, even more secretly, a set I'd seen on sale of *A Vision* and *The Collected Plays of WB Yeats*. I initially regretted the series of decisions and transactions that had deprived me of my vinyl and left me with a headache and these thick tomes full of incomprehensible things. I could make neither head nor tail of *A Vision*, though it all seemed very cool. The symbols and diagrams, at least, seemed resolved, and representative of something, not quite as opaque as the text. I planned tattoos and imagined myself explaining them to girls at parties.

I tried automatic writing but all that appeared was a desultory row of lines of inky peaks and troughs. The plays made far more sense, though the only ones immediately accessible were *Cathleen ni Houlihan* and *The Countess Cathleen*; the former because it had been explained to us in school as an example of allegory, and the latter because it had been mentioned in history class as part of a discussion of the 'good' Famine landlords. Then I came to *On Baile's Strand* and have been haunted by it since. I thought of it the day my son was born.

I tried to write a play but all that appeared on the page was derivative nonsense; there was more meaning and art to the results of my automatic writing attempts. My hero was called Lanad and he took sword against Death and he lashed himself to a tree that he might die on his feet. I burnt it on my bedroom windowsill and resolved to put away the *Collected Plays* and to never open it again.

I was painfully aware of my lack of physical courage as a teenager, and the idea of courage therefore preoccupied me. After I first read 'An Irish Airman Foresees His Death' I was still and silent for a long while, inside and out. Yeats's imagined airman sat in his cockpit among the clouds, a kind of superman, statured and sanctified in my mind, and he tormented me. The pristine nihilism in the closing stanza, the perfect, beautiful courage of it: all that mattered, he declaimed, was the manner of his meeting his fate; nothing before was of any consequence, nothing to come could possibly matter as much. Its military quadrameter pounded out my inadequacy and yet it was my favourite poem. Like Patrick Kavanagh's 'Stony Grey Soil' it forced me to know myself. Yeats described what I was not; Kavanagh what I was.

My father would recite 'The Lake Isle of Innisfree' before rising from the table. As a child I thought he'd made it up himself. I imagined him standing on the forested foreshore at Garrykennedy, composing. He never claimed to have written it; my father has a beautiful soul and such beauty as is in those lines sat easily next to my childish reckoning of him. My father's not the Yeats fan I am, though; he feels that Austin Clarke, one of his heroes, existed and withered in his shadow, and that Kavanagh rightly holds Yeats's title of the greatest of them all.

But as much as I revere Clarke and Kavanagh, and my father, on this we'll always disagree.

Eiléan Ní Chuilleanáin

THE DATE OF EASTER

WB Yeats, *A Full Moon in March* (Macmillan and Co, 1935).

A Full Moon in March is the last of the titled collections of Yeats's poems which he intended to include in the *Collected Poems* he was planning at the time of his death. But the group with that name is not the same collection that appeared in 1935; in fact the title belongs to a play, which is excluded from the *Collected Poems*, along with another, *The King of the Great Clock Tower*, whereas the 1935 volume contained both. A clutch of verse, headed 'Parnell's funeral and other poems', completed the book.

Many of the poems here are spoken by voices which are not the poet's own. They include the songs in the plays, which are distanced from any idea of direct expression. The stage directions prescribe that the characters do not sing, their words are intoned by 'Attendants' who seem to be plucking the poems from the air. The opening exchange of *A Full Moon in March* absolves them of responsibility: 'What do we do? / What part do we take? / What did he say? / [...] "Sing anything, sing any old thing" said he. / "Come then and sing about the dung of swine"'. In the whole book, the voice of Yeats himself, even of his public persona, is intermittently heard and indeed seems to break through with difficulty; when it does, though, it has a particular force.

The two plays have the same plot, *A Full Moon in March* being the later version. A coarse outlaw ('Stranger' or 'Swineherd') demands the love of a queen; he is beheaded for his impertinence but (in *A Full Moon in March*) succeeds in impregnating her when she dances with his severed head: his blood drips on her dress and body and penetrates her. A hinted-at prophecy is perhaps fulfilled; there is also a definite reminiscence of Wilde's *Salome*. Yeats's focus on the connection between orgasm and politics, sexual conjunction and destiny – variously paraded in 'The Second Coming', 'Leda and the Swan' and lesser poems – is framed here as a meeting between the exalted and the earthy, '*Crown of Gold or dung of swine*', a ritual desecration.

There is also a reminiscence of the Christian calendar, which is especially disputatious about the lunar month of March. The Swineherd declares to the Queen that 'You must be won / At a full moon in March'. The feast of the Annunciation, 25 March, falls in the days after the vernal equinox (21 March) and our official date of Easter is on the first Sunday after the full moon that follows that equinox. Thus the impregnation of Queen by Swineherd is aligned with the conception of Christ, each event an overriding of the natural order that announces a new historical epoch, and with resurrection motifs of a dying god reborn. Yeats had studied the disagreements about the date of Easter where the Celts had preferred to follow a different lunar calendar to the Roman church. A defiance of the Christian claim as the sole theological system, a bold foregrounding of sexual compulsiveness, is of a piece with his resolve in the early 1930s to see off any attempt by the Free State Government to censor the activities of the Abbey Theatre.

The plays, in their deliberate artificiality and their focus on aesthetic means, are not in conventional terms *shocking*, but they deal with shock: the shocks of sex, the collisions of opposites. In *The King of the Great Clock Tower* the Second Attendant ('as Queen') sings,

> He longs to kill
> My body, until
> That sudden shudder
> And limbs lie still.

And,

> O, what may come
> Into my womb,
> What caterpillar
> My beauty consume?

Such extremity of feeling runs through the non-dramatic poetry too. The voice we hear is frequently pitched as if addressing an audience but uncertain as to where that audience can be found. It mostly lacks the authoritative tone of *The Tower* and *The Winding Stair* – of such resolute and humanly involved poems as 'Coole Park, 1929' and 'Coole Park and Ballylee, 1931', of such fantastic and fertile imaginative excursions as 'Leda and the Swan' and the Byzantium pieces. A simple explanation for such apparent faltering is the death of Lady Gregory in 1932 and the consequent loss of Coole – not just as a lifelong refuge but as the scene of a national literary project, stretching back thirty years and more before the foundation of the state in which he now finds himself – having resigned from the Senate at the time of his serious illness in 1928 – in a diminished public capacity.

There is a continuity, certainly, in the deliberate outrageousness of the plays and the cultivated wildness of several of the poems in *A Full Moon in March*, with the Crazy Jane who spoke out in *The Winding Stair,* and with Yeats's determined resistance, in the Senate and elsewhere, to the Censorship of Publications Act of 1929. His search broadens, for alternative voicings of ideas that are his and not quite his own. He has always aimed for a public resonance and here he makes himself heard in a variety of ways. The public voice of an orator aiming to persuade, and the voice of a quasi-anonymous song writer aiming to put words into the mouths of others, alternate with the voice of a poet meditating on history and humanity – the voice of Yeats that sounds most serious and that we are most likely to listen to.

More shocking for many modern readers than any breach of religious or sexual taboos is his admiration for Italian fascism which in the spring of 1933 saw him drawn into the conservative reaction to de Valera's re-election at the head of a majority government. Among the forces that emerged from the panic-stricken right wing were the 'para-fascist' (Roy Foster's expression) Blueshirts. Yeats's ideal of 'government of the educated classes' was not quite what their leader O'Duffy was after, with his emphasis on race and religion. Still, Yeats wrote three marching songs for the Blueshirts, though he retreated almost immediately from the con-nection and revised the songs. They are strange pieces, where 'marching' for its own sake is countered by ironic refrains: '"Drown all the dogs," said the fierce young woman, / "They killed my goose and a cat."' I prefer that to 'Time for us all to pick out a good tune, / Take to the roads and go marching along. / March, march – how does it run? – / O any old words to a tune.' Yeats noted, of his revisions, 'I increased their fantasy, their extravagance, their obscurity, that no party might sing them.' What's surprising is that he allowed them to survive at all, but they are the extreme example of the oddity of this volume.

In 'Parnell's Funeral' we hear the magisterial poetic voice, the voice of earlier political poems – 'Easter 1916' or 'The Stare's Nest', say – without the rattle of the marchers' drum. The message remains anti-democratic. Parnell is the tragic leader, contrasted with the 'Great Comedian' O'Connell, and with the figures thrown up by the history of Ireland: de Valera, Cosgrave and 'even O'Duffy', 'Their school a crowd, his master solitude.' His grandiloquence does not hide what is most characteristic of Yeats: a sense of responsibility and of his inability to meet that respon-sibility without some manipulation of metaphor – which the reader may experience as an excavation of the emotions surrounding Parnell's fate that moves towards the truth of what really happened.

> None shared our guilt; nor did we play a part
> Upon a painted stage when we devoured his heart.

More acute perhaps in its political perception is the briefer 'Church and State', where he asks what looks like, with hindsight, the right question about the Ireland of the 1930s: 'What if the Church and the State / Are the mob that howls at the door!'

Succeeding the single 'songs', with their provisional-sounding titles ('Alternative Song for the Severed Head', 'Two Songs Rewritten for the Tune's Sake'), and 'A Prayer for Old Age', the volume concludes with an extraordinary series of 'Supernatural Songs'. Yeats imagines a pre-Patrician Christian hermit, Ribh, whose Christianity comes 'perhaps from Egypt like much early Irish Christianity', and declares grandly 'I did not explain the poems in *The King of the Great Clock Tower* nor will I explain [the Supernatural Songs].' Ribh the hermit argues, against the sexless Trinity of St Patrick, that 'As man, as beast, as an ephemeral fly begets, Godhead begets Godhead'; he turns the pages of his holy book by the light generated from the posthumous coupling of the legendary lovers Baile and Aillinn. Later political epochs inaugurate through the same energy: 'What sacred drama through her body heaved / When world-transforming Charlemagne was conceived?' But there is a corresponding destructive force, mankind 'despite his terror, cannot cease / Ravening through century after century, / Ravening, raging, and uprooting that he may come / Into the desolation of reality'. Through Ribh, who is not a mask for Yeats, we access a calm, terrible contemplation of a totality of creation and its undoing. Not only is it much more impressive than his vision of political anarchy, it is a view of life and fate that only his own life experience and his strange intellectual adventures could have offered him, and the reader's privilege is to share that revelation.

WB Yeats

LONG-LEGGED FLY

That civilisation may not sink,
Its great battle lost,
Quiet the dog, tether the pony
To a distant post.
Our master Caesar is in the tent
Where the maps are spread,
His eyes fixed upon nothing,
A hand upon his head.

Like a long-legged fly upon the stream
His mind moves upon silence.

That the topless towers be burnt
And men recall that face,
Move most gently if move you must
In this lonely place.
She thinks, part woman, three parts a child,
That nobody looks; her feet
Practise a tinker shuffle
Picked up on the street.

Like a long-legged fly upon the stream
Her mind moves upon silence.

That girls at puberty may find
The first Adam in their thought,
Shut the door of the Pope's chapel,
Keep those children out.
There on that scaffolding reclines
Michael Angelo.
With no more sound than the mice make
His hand moves to and fro.

Like a long-legged fly upon the stream
His mind moves upon silence.

Jeffrey Wainwright

THE KEEPERS

That civilisation may not sink
Down the slope, beneath the walls,
Through ragged orchards, plots undug,
Then capture water, capture water.

As it stumbles from the rock devise
Some trays of stone, pipes of copper or of clay,
Carry it level by engine or by hand
To cisterns dank but safe beneath the town.

Be jealous of any sip a lizard seeks,
Any larceny by snake or bird,
Any draught denied our rightful corn.
What can we be but keepers of our own?

WB Yeats

A DEEP-SWORN VOW

Others because you did not keep
That deep-sworn vow have been friends of mine;
Yet always when I look death in the face,
When I clamber to the heights of sleep,
Or when I grow excited with wine,
Suddenly I meet your face.

Alice Lyons

DEEP-SWORN

Others because you did not keep.
Paltry years of gleaning
in the fields of others' mothers
ceased when your field fell to me.
It was the feast of Thanksgiving.

'Dead' is an old word with a face.
Not 'passed away', nor 'put to sleep', not _____.
You kept out, kept away, kept from.
I'd have curled up on your deathbed
like a dog we were that deep-sworn.

Yet always in the pantry of preserves
jam-jars of jewel light keeping innermost
lemons, littlenecks, beetroot, quince
or when aproned we open up the *Joy of Cooking*
suddenly I meet your face.

Blake Morrison

INFATUATION

I became addicted to Yeats during a fifteen-month spell in Canada. In my undergraduate years, he'd more or less passed me by; I knew Auden's elegy for him better than his for Major Gregory; I knew (and resented) his dismissal of Wilfred Owen's war poetry ('all blood, dirt and sucked sugar stick') better than 'An Irish Airman Foresees His Death' or 'Easter 1916'. Then he appeared in the dead of winter, amid the snows of Ontario. I was taking English 731, an MA seminar course at McMaster University run by an inspiring Welsh lecturer called Brian John. For a term we'd looked at Blake and his Prophetic Books. In January we turned to Yeats, gradually moving away from a path even I knew to be well-worn – the Abbey, the influence of Pound, the relationship with Maud Gonne, etc. – to the later Crazy Jane poems and *A Vision*.

A Vision! A book that's mad as the mist and snow. One of the maddest ever written. Certainly the maddest written by Yeats. Privately published in 1925, it came out again, with revisions, in 1937. His introduction describes how it began:

> On the afternoon of October 24th 1917, four days after my marriage, my wife surprised me by attempting automatic writing. What came in disjointed sentences, in almost illegible writing, was so exciting, sometimes so profound, that I persuaded her to give an hour or two day after day to the unknown writer, and after some half-dozen such hours offered to spend what remained of life explaining and piecing together those scattered sentences.

The piecing together took Yeats years. He'd have a pencil and paper ready whenever 'they', the mysterious instructors, put George in a trance, and he'd ask them questions, the answers to which often lay in geometrical symbols. Other hauntings occurred to convince Yeats he was in the presence of spiritual guides: strange smells, flashes of light, whistlings, and 'still stranger phenomena that I prefer to remain silent about'. As well as the good guys, aka instructors, there were bad guys, aka frustrators, who'd confuse or undo the communication process. But by 1920, Yeats had fifty copy-books to help him evolve his system, 'a last act of defence against the chaos of the world'.

My US paperback edition of *A Vision* and my hardback of the *Collected Poems* are both covered with earnest marginalia and underlinings from that time. Looking over them today, I feel as embarrassed as I do remembering the night I spooked myself at a Ouija board. But at McMaster we students pored over *A Vision* like code-breakers at Bletchley, as though by cracking its system – the gyres, the phases of the moon, the anti-self, the great wheel, the historical cones – we'd achieve some ultimate knowledge: Truth, Peace, God, Spiritual Enlightenment, the kind of transcendence more usually sought through drugs, which we were taking too, though not in Dr John's seminar. I say 'we', but it may just have been me who lost my head that winter.

Lost my head but found a poet. Joyce regretted that Yeats didn't put the findings of *A Vision* 'into a creative work', but he did. 'We have come to give you metaphors for poetry', the ghostly instructors tell him, and the governing motifs and ideas of *A Vision* are present in many of his greatest poems, including 'The Second Coming', 'A Prayer for my Daughter', 'Among School Children', 'Sailing to Byzantium' and 'Under Ben Bulben'. The source material may be impenetrable, even to occultists. But as Yeats said, the muses sometimes form their most lasting attachments in low haunts. Or as he puts it in 'Crazy Jane Talks with the Bishop', echoing Blake's line in Jerusalem 'I will make their places of joy and love, excrementitious':

> 'But Love has pitched his mansion in
> The place of excrement;
> For nothing can be sole or whole
> That has not been rent.'

The rending expressed in *A Vision* is that of a man torn between two alter egos (Michael Robartes vs. Owen Aherne), whose mind muddles astrology and history, the occult and the oracular, the numinous and the numerical. Perhaps that's why it appealed to me, divided as I felt (between home and away, Europe and North America, old and new) while also believing that division was healthy. But it may just have been the excellence of that seminar and of a lecture I heard Denis Donoghue give on Yeats in Montreal. I ended the course with a long essay on Yeats's concept of frenzy. The downside of this frenzy was fanaticism, even fascism: 'Love war because of its horror,' he wrote in *On the Boiler*, 'that belief may be changed, civilization renewed.' But I didn't hold the fanaticism against him; I was too much of a fan.

I came back from Canada on a Polish liner called the *Stefan Batory*. For most of the ten-day voyage I lay seasick in my cabin writing sub-Yeatsian verses. Home again but new to London, I dispatched them to A. Alvarez at the *Observer*, whence they quickly came back. Then I discovered Larkin and the Movement rationalists. Larkin got Yeats out of his system by reading Hardy; I got Yeats out of my system by reading Larkin. The infatuation with *A Vision* was over. An attachment to the best of Yeats remains.

Hugo Hamilton

BESCHEIDENHEIT

We were too young perhaps. We did, of course, understand Yeats at
school. We examined his poetry, discussed his 'fisherman' and felt we got
his meaning. But we may have been too young to comprehend his
intentions fully. We knew how to answer the questions we were asked.
Why the poet could feel so let down by Ireland, by time, by the nature of
things not remaining intact the way he saw them. We could write essays
about his disheartened view, why he felt as unrequited in his private love
as he did in his love for his country. We understood the energy of his
words and adopted his phrases, accused each other of making jokes
'aimed at the commonest ear', dismissed the clever among us as having
nothing to offer but the 'the catch cries of the clown'.

We appreciated the poet's admiration for the fisherman in his 'grey
Connemara clothes'. We knew that 'sun freckled face'. We knew the
longing Yeats had for perfection, for the uncomplicated nobility of the
fisherman. Fishermen had cool. Their simplicity told us something about
ourselves, though we did not understand until now that Yeats was
looking at the Connemara fisherman in the way we might look at
someone in the least developed nations of the world today.

We came from a generation lucky enough to hear that fisherman in
person, speaking Connemara Irish. We could visually imagine him 'cast
his flies' onto the stream, with the 'down turn' of his hand. Though later,
we revised our innocent reading of it when it came to our attention that
casting flies was not the activity of a Connemara fisherman, but the
sport of gentry. No Connemara man that I knew ever went fishing with
a rod. I saw them in boats, I saw them with lobster pots, I saw them
poaching salmon in the river by night with a spear, a gaff, never a rod.

Fine. We were ready to make allowances for poetic idealism. We
understood the latitude of art. The truth is 'cold and passionate' as the
dawn, it does not require extreme fact-checking.

Here is the fisherman we saw with our own eyes. *An Cheathrú Rua*,
Carraroe, Connemara, Co Galway – 1959. Walking back from the beach
along '*an bóthar buí*' (the yellow road) with my mother. It begins to rain.
We take shelter in a fisherman's house. The woman of the house has no
English, my German mother has no Irish. So there is no communication
between them – only smiles, silence, that shyness between languages.
The house is full of fishing equipment. Grey fishing nets draped over the
banisters. When the fisherman comes in, he looks at my mother for a
long time, so my mother records in her diary, as though he's trying to
work out where he might have seen her before:

Er schaute mich an als ob er mich kannte.
He looked at me as though he recognized me.

He treats her not as a stranger but as a woman from another parish within walking distance, a woman he should know and cannot quite place. And she sees in him something that she admires. *Bescheidenheit*, is the word she keeps repeating to us, because she wants us to learn his ability to live without avarice, not to become grabbers.

Reading the Yeats poem at school, it clicked right away. That's him. I passed it on to my mother and she instantly recognized the fisherman we had met in Carraroe, the man whose wife waved us in out of the rain. Years later, I went back there and found the house empty, one or two lobster pots left outside.

Maybe the Yeats poem cannot be fully understood by a schoolboy. Some poetry only reaches the adult in you. Now I understand it differently, perhaps it is the poet who has become the stranger here, the visitor, like my mother. She had that same reporter's role, couldn't wait to tell her sisters back home in Germany, that need to make sense of the place and all its misunderstandings, all those things about to disappear.

A man who does not exist,
A man who is but a dream …

The poet's gaze is the problem, Yeats clearly knows that. The onlooker is the loser. As soon as we record the fisherman in words, he turns into a dream, an imaginary being who begins to outlive the living. It's not only late romantic idealism that presents us with a question here but the very nature of external description, projecting, viewing the other from outside. Yeats, like most writers, is describing something in the fisherman that is missing in himself.

Or was he an environmentalist? Was he saving the fisherman from corruption, from becoming the stereotype of a fisherman? Was he blessed or cursed for having seen the real man, forced to find words to keep him intact and protect him from extinction?

It was not until much later that I became aware of the poet's brush with the fascist vision, if that's what it really was. My father's post-independence generation had a similar longing to keep things in Ireland from disappearing. In spite of marrying a German woman and starting a cross-cultural family in Dublin, he idealized the self-sufficiency of the fisherman. He didn't want him getting tainted by outside influences, particularly British. Like so many others charged with the post-colonial duty of shaping a new Ireland, my father fell into the self-colonial trap of isolation, he had the poet's ideological preservation order on the simple Irishman:

All day I'd looked in the face
What I had hoped 'twould be
To write for my own race ...

There is something in the fisherman poem that we never discussed at
school. 'My own race', what does that mean? Race? The word never even
came up, though it is there, tucked neatly into the lines. Where do we
stand here, with our mongrel identity? Is Yeats speaking for us? Tell me,
is he talking about difference, specialness, purity?

Is it right to ask those questions now, so late? Is it right for me to
wonder if a contemporary fisherman from the shores of Senegal would
recognize himself in that Yeats poem? Would an inward migrant identify
with it?

Beware of applying knowledge backwards, that's all I can say. We
judge with such ease what is behind us, we feel so grown-up now. Our
post-Auschwitz intelligence makes the past look so childish, so blinded in
its allegiance to beauty. How could Yeats, of all people, not predict that
we would outgrow this cult of exceptionalism? We're gone global now,
people on the move everywhere. There is no advantage left in purity. Or
perhaps this is exactly what the great poet is trying to anticipate,
posthumously, that the pure Irishman, the pure fisherman, might become
a thing of the past. And we're not to worry about it.

Adrian Frazier

The Maud Gonne Crossword
Just names and numbers

ACROSS

2 Women's nationalist organization she founded.
4 Nationalist weekly that she bankrolled.
7 Both Yeats and Maud Gonne spent childhood months here.
9 The head of the IRB, who swore her in as a member.
10 This lover was a founder of the Ligue antisemitique.
12 Her dear Paris friend, a French poet and author of 'Ode to the Vagina.'
14 She tried to conceive her second child in this first child's tomb.
15 Before she met Yeats, this Irishman fell for her.
17 She was born here, near the Aldershot Barracks.
18 First name of her half-sister, a baby at the time of Colonel Gonne's death.
19 The IRB not being sufficiently active, she joined this secret nationalist organization.
20 Coastal village in Normandy near where Yeats and Gonne summered.
21 At this event, 30,000 Dublin children were served buns, candy, and soft drinks.

DOWN

1 Present name and function of the place her father died.
3 Maternal grandfather, one of the richest men in England.
5 City where the poet was rewarded for his long devotion, alas, 'when Time had touched her form.'
6 Her height was at at least....
8 Cousin on her father's side, and, in 'Adam's Curse,' explained that it was difficult to be beautiful.
11 Honeymoon destination, in order to place a bomb on visiting Edward VII.
13 She always forgot she went to school here.
16 City where she met her husband Major MacBride.

Answers on page 200

Paul Muldoon

CIRCUS ATTRACTIONS

WB Yeats, *Last Poems and Two Plays* (Cuala Press, 1939).

This posthumous volume by WB Yeats, his thirteenth, is a book that will confirm his reputation as one of the great poets of the English language. The range of his work is rather handily outlined in 'The Circus Animals' Desertion,' a *tour d'horizon* of his 'old themes'. Part of Yeats's great gift has been to reconcile his innate hauteur, his 'High Talk,' his 'stilted' language, with the commonplace image:

> Those masterful images because complete
> Grew in pure mind, but out of what began?
> A mound of refuse or the sweepings of a street,
> Old kettles, old bottles, and a broken can,
> Old iron, old bones, old rags, that raving slut
> Who keeps the till. Now that my ladder's gone,
> I must lie down where all the ladders start
> In the foul rag and bone shop of the heart.

Yeats here manages to combine a reference to the Music Hall star Harry Champion's great song, 'Any Old Iron,' recorded in 1935 on EMI with the orchestra of the London Palladium, and the 'ladder' imagery associated with philosophers as diverse as Plato, Hegel, and most recently Wittgenstein, who writes in *Tractatus* 6.54, first published in English in 1922:

> My propositions are elucidatory in this way: he who understands me
> finally recognizes them as senseless, when he has climbed out through
> them, on them, over them. (He must so to speak throw away the ladder,
> after he has climbed up on it).
>
> He must surmount these propositions; then he sees the world rightly.

Yeats's ambition to see the world 'rightly' has led him to take what many have seen as a wrong turn, nowhere more memorably than in *A Vision*. As recently as last year, in the summer 1938 number of the *Yale Review,* Kerker Quinn was bold enough to assert:

> Mr Yeats's new volumes will convince many that he has gone
> unquestionably, though perhaps serviceably, mad, without awaiting the
> permission he asked of us in a recent poem:

> Grant me an old man's frenzy.
> Myself must I remake
> Till I am Timon and Lear
> Or that William Blake
> Who beat upon the wall
> Till Truth obeyed his call ...

> Yet, like Blake's prophetic poems, they plentifully repay even those
> readers who feel incapable of or uninterested in following him to such
> truth as may be hidden deep in myth and mysticism.

'Myth and mysticism' abound in *Last Poems*, including the first piece,
'Under Ben Bulben', in which we're put on our mettle from the outset:

> Swear by what the Sages spoke
> Round the Mareotic Lake
> That the Witch of Atlas knew,
> Spoke and set the cocks a-crow.

The difficulty of Yeats's work has become a byword. The 'Mareotic Lake'
will remain a mystery for many readers, though some may be familiar
with the terrain from 'Demon and Beast' in *Michael Robartes and the
Dancer* (1921):

> O what a sweetness strayed
> Through barren Thebaid,
> Or by the Mareotic sea
> When that exultant Anthony
> And twice a thousand more
> Starved upon the shore
> And withered to a bag of bones!
> What had the Caesars but their thrones?

When we come to understand that the Mareotic sea, near Alexandria in
Egypt, was an area associated with Christian monasticism in the fourth
century, the era also of the Stylite or 'pillar-saint' in the early Byzantine
empire, things may begin to fall into place. The most famous stylite,
Simeon, lived on top of his pillar near Aleppo for thirty-seven years – a
little longer, it must be said, than Yeats spent in Thoor Ballylee! Such is
the continuity of Yeats's world view, however, that the 'Stylite' is
etymologically linked to the 'stilt' of 'High Talk':

Malachi Stilt-Jack am I, whatever I learned has run wild,
From collar to collar, from stilt to stilt, from father to child.
All metaphor, Malachi, stilts and all. A barnacle goose
Far up in the stretches of night ...

I will leave it to another generation of critics to determine the significance of the propinquity of the words 'Malachi,' so inextricably related to the character of James Joyce's Malachi Mulligan, a version of Yeats's friend, Oliver St John Gogarty, author of the recent collection of poems *Elbow Room* (1939), and the maiden name of Joyce's wife, Nora *Barnacle*. (Perhaps Yeats is acknowledging the influence of the 'modern' Joyce on his 'mound of refuse or the sweepings of the street?'). In the meantime, I will point to the intricate connections between 'a bag of bones' in 'Demon and Beast' and the 'old bones' in 'The Circus Animals' Desertion', between the ascetic impulse of 'exultant Anthony' the Great, the Egyptian Desert Father, and Yeats's own ascetic impulse to 'lie down where all the ladders start', between the 'Caesars' and 'their thrones' and the Caesar of 'Long-Legged Fly':

That civilization may not sink
Its great battle lost,
Quiet the dog, tether the pony
To a distant post.
Our master Caesar is in the tent
Where the maps are spread,
His eyes fixed upon nothing,
A hand under his head.

Like a long-legged fly upon the stream
His mind moves upon silence.

Yeats is not only a masterful image-maker but a masterful *self*-image maker, that 'long-legged fly' connecting him not only to the 'Daddy-long-legs' of 'High Talk' but Michael Angelo 'there on the scaffolding'. Yeats's family is a family of visual artists, his brother Jack B Yeats having distinguished himself as an illustrator of life in the Big Top. It is not, surely, too much to suggest that the 'Jack' in 'Malachi Stilt-*Jack*' is a version of the poet's own brother, particularly when we find him in such propinquity to the 'piebald ponies, led bears, caged lions'. Those 'piebald ponies' include the 'pony' tethered 'to a distant post' from 'Long-Legged Fly' while the lineage of the 'dog' in that poem may be traced at least as far back as 'The Tower' of 1928:

What shall I do with this absurdity –
O heart, O troubled heart – this caricature,
Decrepit age that has been tied to me
As to a dog's tail?
                                    Never had I more
Excited, passionate, fantastical
Imagination, nor an ear and eye
That more expected the impossible –
No, not in boyhood when with rod and fly,
Or the humbler worm, <u>I climbed Ben Bulben's back</u>
And had the livelong summer day to spend.
It seems that I must bid the Muse go pack,
Choose Plato and Plotinus for a friend
Until imagination, ear and eye,
Can be content with argument and deal
In abstract things; or be derided by
A sort of battered kettle at the heel.

Yet again, we find ourselves in a dizzying gyre of image refracting image, the 'battered kettle at the heel' of the dog anticipating the 'old kettles' in 'The Circus Animals' Desertion' while 'the livelong [summer] day' conjures up the most famous use of that phrase by Murellus in *Julius Caesar*:

Wherefore rejoice? What conquest brings he home?
What tributaries follow him to Rome
To grace in captive bonds his chariot wheels?
You blocks, you stones, you worse than senseless things!
O you hard hearts, you cruel men of Rome,
Knew you not Pompey? Many a time and oft
Have you climbed up to walls and battlements,
To towers and windows, yea, to chimney tops,
Your infants in your arms, and there have sat
The livelong day, with patient expectation,
To see great Pompey pass the streets of Rome.

That passage anticipates not only 'Caesar in his tent' in 'Long-legged Fly' but, in its shared vocabulary – 'chariot,' 'stones' and 'hearts' – 'The Circus Animals' Desertion.'

The 'Ben Bulben's back' that the poet climbed in 'The Tower' has now taken a central place in his iconography. It's a place that embodies more than any other Yeats's capacity to synthesize. 'Under Ben Bulben' takes in not only the Mareotic Lake and Shelley's 'The Witch of Atlas' but the Fianna and Phidias, John Mitchel and Michael Angelo (again!), gyres and 'hard-riding country gentlemen'. It's a poem that may, however, spread itself a little too thin in its attempt to cover so much. There will be some readers who will remain unconvinced that the doggerel of 'Irish poets, learn your trade / Sing whatever is well made, / Scorn the sort now growing up / All out of shape from toe to top' is the kind of writing to which the next generation of Irish versifiers should aspire. They will learn much more from Yeats's own aspiration to 'remake' himself, an aspiration nonetheless tempered by his exasperation at the fact he is doomed to 'enumerate old themes'. What made Yeats so successful, right up to the end, was his remarkable capacity to enter the ring with a foot on the back of each of these two horses.

Geraldine Higgins

NEWS THAT STAYS NEW: THE FUTURE LIFE OF WB YEATS

Towards the end of his life, Yeats asked to be buried in Sligo, 'when the newspapers have forgotten me'. Anticipating our modern line that today's news wraps tomorrow's fish and chips, he thinks of newspapers as ephemeral, poetry as eternal. In fact, few poets have enjoyed such a long afterlife in the news media as WB Yeats and indeed newspapers as we know them are likely to be forgotten long before we forget him. Yeats had a complicated relationship with newspapers and news editors in his lifetime, raging against the ignorance of the press while assiduously promoting his own causes. Reflecting on his engagement with the news, Yeats writes, 'In the thirty years or so during which I have been reading Irish newspapers, three public controversies have stirred my imagination.' These three public controversies – over Parnell, Synge's *The Playboy of the Western World* and the Hugh Lane Gallery – have subsequently received a great deal of critical attention in Yeats scholarship. However, the ratio of three public issues in thirty years rather disingenuously asserts Yeats's artistic disengagement from the daily news.

Yeats, an inveterate letter-writer, courted the attention of certain newspaper editors and successfully alienated others. Daniel Albright calls the title poem of Yeats's collection, *In the Seven Woods*, the first in which the poet is 'obviously a man who reads the newspaper': 'I have forgot awhile / Tara uprooted, and new commonness / Upon the throne'. More often Yeats treats the news business with the same scorn he shows for the whiff of the shop, remembering 'the dirty piece of orange-peel in the corner of the stairs as one climbs up to some newspaper office'.

So what do we make of the fact that WB Yeats has become the poet of choice for journalists, news editors, and politicians in our own time? In Ireland, the first female president, Mary Robinson, invited the audience at her inauguration to 'Come dance with me in Ireland', invoking an inclusive Yeats as the symbol of her pluralist Presidency. Her successor, Mary McAleese echoed Yeats's wish for a future in which 'Everything we look upon is blest'. In fact, Yeats's words continue to appear in new and surprising contexts, demonstrating his appeal not only to Irish commentators, but also to journalists and politicians on platforms across the globe.

Obviously the journalists, politicians, and speech-writers who quote Yeats intend to display a literariness or concern for the craft of wielding language that raises the rhetorical level of each speech. But what does this kind of engagement say about the relationship between the political and the poetic? And, what do such moments tell us about Yeats, particularly the Yeats who said in 1935, 'I have always been a propagandist though I have kept it out of my poems'. Perhaps the most salutary moment to begin with is Edith Wharton's request that Yeats produce an anti-war poem for her 1916 anthology, *The Book of the Homeless*. In his somewhat churlish response, 'On Being asked for a War Poem', Yeats takes the opportunity to reprimand poets who get involved in politics:

> I think it better that in times like these
> A poet's mouth be silent, for in truth
> We have no gift to set a statesman right;
> He has had enough of meddling who can please
> A young girl in the indolence of her youth,
> Or an old man upon a winter's night.

Yeats of course was not averse to setting statesmen right when it suited him and indeed became a statesman himself in 1922. According to Derek Mahon, 'A good poem is a paradigm of good politics – of people talking to each other, with honest subtlety at a profound level.' Much debate has taken place about the intersection between poetry and politics but here I will focus on three familiar Yeats poems – 'The Lake Isle of Innisfree', 'The Second Coming', and 'September 1913' – and three different occasions when these poems were quoted at crucial moments in the contemporary period.

PEACE COMES DROPPING SLOW

WB Yeats was an island-hopper. In the days before residency requirements meant counting every day spent 'outside the jurisdiction', Yeats was legitimately a resident of Ireland and England with a series of addresses that indicate for scholars his social class as well as his cultural aspirations. As Roy Foster puts it: 'In his shabby but atmospheric rooms in Woburn Buildings, conveniently and symbolically situated between the British Museum (for intellectual inspiration) and Euston Station (for the boat-train to Ireland), WBY contrived to entertain literary and artistic Bohemia.' The Museum and the Station situate Yeats in a geography of the metropole and colony within which his literary and artistic Bohemia is an island of his own making.

Of course it is Sligo rather than the London of Bedford Park and Woburn Buildings that claimed the poet's loyalty: 'I longed … for earth from a road there that I might kiss it'. Nonetheless, the island with which WBY is most intimately associated, the Lake Isle of Innisfree, owes as much to London as to Sligo for its poetic conception. Yeats was so excited about writing 'The Lake Isle of Innisfree' that he burst into the

drawing room to read it to his sisters and called it 'my first lyric with anything in its rhythm of my own music'.

The poem, written 'in exile' in London, was inspired by a little
fountain advertising 'cooling drinks' in a shop-window on the Strand but
Yeats eliminates this trigger from the poem and reduces London only to
its 'pavements grey'. Indeed, in his letters to Katharine Tynan from
London in the 1880s, Yeats identifies with literature's most famous
castaway, saying, 'I feel like Robinson Crusoe in this dreadful London',
and later writes, 'here I am stranded for I know not how long in this
London desert'. For the poet, Innisfree and London are island opposites,
one the dreamy location of an idealized artistic solitude and the other,
the metropolis of alienation and exile. Yeats's Innisfree is not only his
best-known poem; it is also the Mecca of 'Yeats Country' in Sligo – the
place where tourists assemble to experience the purple glow of peace
and tranquility.

In 2013, Northern Ireland celebrated fifteen years of the peace sealed
by the Good Friday agreement in 1998. Writing in the *New York Times*,
Colum McCann began his article, 'Remembering an Easter Miracle in
Northern Ireland' by quoting the familiar line, '"Peace", said WB Yeats,
"comes dropping slow"'. He goes on to marvel at the fact that:

> After 15 years, the Good Friday peace agreement in Northern Ireland
> still occasionally quivers, sometimes abruptly, and yet it holds. It is one
> of the great stories of the second half of the 20th century, and by the
> nature of its refusal to topple, it is one of the continuing marvels of the
> 21st as well. While rockets fizzle across the Israeli border, and funeral
> chants sound along the streets of Aleppo in Syria, and drones cut
> coordinates in the blue over Kandahar, Afghanistan, the Irish peace
> process reaffirms the possibility that – despite the weight of evidence
> against human nature – we are all still capable of small moments of
> resurrection, no matter where we happen to be.

McCann's article reaffirms Northern Ireland's position as the great
success story of conflict resolution, the place that offers hope to the
ancient antagonists in Israel, Aleppo and Kandahar. In situating the Good
Friday Agreement in the realm of Easter miracles, McCann not only
nods to the 1916 Rising, but also elevates this 'small moment of
resurrection' to the mythical rather than political realm of possibility.
The new co-ordinates of the Good Friday Agreement mean that bombs
no longer burst in air across the Irish border, instead, peace comes
dropping slow.

In opening his article with this particular quotation, McCann is
probably unaware that one of the architects of the Good Friday
agreement, David Trimble, did the same thing fifteen years previously. The

day after being informed that he and John Hume had just been awarded the Nobel Peace Prize, David Trimble wrote an article for *The Observer* which began by quoting the same line from 'The Lake Isle of Innisfree'. 'Peace comes dropping slow', said Mr Trimble, 'Northern Ireland is slowly moving towards peace. Too slowly.' He went on to talk about the need for decommissioning weapons and minds before berating certain begrudgers 'who cannot lift their eyes from this month's sectarian dogfight to observe the promising vista unfolding for Northern Ireland as peace and prosperity take hold, and as the taint of political rancour and violence give way to international goodwill'. Significantly, Trimble finished the article with another reference to Ireland's first poet Laureate: 'But American investment and a peace prize will not add up to more than Yeats's nine bean-rows on the Isle of Innisfree without a change of outlook on both extremes.'

Trimble's use of the nine bean-rows nicely bookends his article with Yeats, echoing his 'peace comes dropping slow' at the beginning of the piece. At first, Yeats provides him with an ironic quip which relies on the audience recognizing the reference without necessarily knowing the poem. However, with the second quotation, Trimble shows that he is reading the poem against the grain – he dismisses the nine bean-rows as a 'hill of beans', a hopeless harvest for those who trust to money and prizes instead of the harder currency of decommissioned weapons. So, when he returns to Yeats's 'nine bean-rows' at the end of the article, he transplants them as an image of deficiency rather than the ascetic sufficiency suggested in the poem – 'Nine bean-rows will I have there, a hive for the honey-bee, / And live alone in the bee-loud glade'.

Despite its associations with a boat journey, nostalgia and escape from temporal concerns, the poem seems tethered to the dock of politics in its subsequent iterations. In 2013, speaking in Belfast, President Obama quoted Yeats in his assessment of the long journey towards peace before and after the Good Friday Agreement: 'Yeats once wrote "Peace comes dropping slow". But that doesn't mean our efforts to forge a real and lasting peace should come dropping slow. This work is as urgent now as it has ever been, because there's more to lose now than there has ever been.' President Obama's speechwriters have also updated his database of quotable Irish writers not just by adding Seamus Heaney but also newer writers like Colum McCann. After quoting the Yeats line 'Peace comes dropping slow', in this speech, President Obama said: '"Peace is indeed harder than war", the Irish author Colum McCann recently wrote, "and its constant fragility is part of its beauty. A bullet need happen only once, but for peace to work we need to be reminded of its existence again and again and again."' The poetic line from 'The Lake Isle of Innisfree' becomes an opportunity to meditate on the idea and idealism of peace as well as the pragmatic efforts needed to maintain it. Yeats's words are woven into the discussions, debates and speeches of the peace process because he seems to address our times directly, his words resonating with current events, showing the power of news that stays new.

THE CENTRE CANNOT HOLD

It is worth remembering the work, the pressure and the hope invested in the peace process as well as the many many words it took to reach agreement. President Clinton visited Ireland three times in the 1990s during the crucial period leading up to the Good Friday agreement of 1998. In preparation, he pored over Irish books and briefings which staffers had prepared for him, including a slim volume of poems by William Butler Yeats. Clinton recalls, 'When I was going to Ireland, I read a lot of Yeats, again, especially the poems that were written around the time of the Irish civil war to try to get a feel for it and also because it's wonderful poetry'. At his most important keynote address in Belfast, outlining the possibilities of the future for a peaceful North, Clinton referred to Yeats's most quoted poem:

> And to the people of Northern Ireland, I say that it is your will for peace that has brought your country to this moment of hope. Do not let it slip away. It will not come again in our lifetime. Give your leaders the support they need to make the hard, but necessary decisions. With apologies to Mr Yeats, help them to prove that things can come together, that the centre can hold.

Clinton is far from being the first politician to find in Yeats's poem a quotable image of millennial anxiety and despair, but here he translates Yeats's apocalyptic vision into a victory for unity rather than fragmentation, for co-operation rather than terror. Theorist David Harvey elects 'Things fall apart; the centre cannot hold; / Mere anarchy is loosed upon the world' as *the* epigraph of the twentieth century and indeed Yeats's modernist anxiety about the centre 'holding' has become political and cultural shorthand for the need for compromise and consensus.

Nonetheless, something has changed since I first began cataloging such usages of 'The Second Coming' in political discourse. In the 1990s, columnist William Safire suggested that 'The Second Coming' was cited with such reckless abandon that it should be retired as a soundbite source. With even greater force, publisher Niall O'Dowd claimed that lines such as 'A terrible beauty is born' or 'The centre cannot hold' or 'Too long a sacrifice can make a stone of the heart' were used by American politicians 'who think they're very clever using them', but, he said, 'people in Ireland would see that and say, "Oh that's almost the equivalent of blarney at this stage"'. Such lines, he implied, had been drained of political currency by overuse and now functioned almost as clichés or dead metaphors. More recently, the journalists and politicians who quote Yeats, particularly with reference to the Iraq war, feel obliged to undercut the force of the quotation by acknowledging its clichéd status.

Ghazi Salahuddin, writing in *The News International* of the uncertain future of Pakistan wrote, 'So much more has happened during the week to confirm, as Yeats had said, that "things fall apart; the centre cannot hold". I know that this quotation has become a cliché ... I remember reading an entire article on this linkage in *The New York Times* earlier this year.' In fact, the article he refers to, is Adam Cohen's February 2007 piece in *The New York Times* called 'What WB Yeats's Second Coming Really Says About the Iraq War' and it begins by telling us that the Brookings Institution entitled their report on the Iraq War, 'Things Fall Apart'. Cohen claims that those who quote 'The Second Coming' with reference to Iraq are 'picking up on Yeats's words, but not his world view'. Cohen turns to Helen Vendler for his reading of the poem and points out that it is 'really two poems'. The first eight lines are the most quotable, but, as Cohen argues, 'the second, less quoted part is the one that speaks most directly to the grim situation in Iraq'.

In Yeats's cyclical system of thought, the 'rough beast' ... slouching towards Bethlehem' is the annunciation of a new cycle with its own pinnacle of civilization, a necessary oppositional gyre to the democratic Christian phase of history. Critics argue whether the 'rough beast' is an analogy for the IRA or the Black and Tans, the Bolshevist revolutionaries or the rise of the Fascists. Likewise, Yeatsian scholars debate about the balance of terror and fascination in the poem – does Yeats long for this apocalypse or dread the violence of its annunciation? In 1936, Yeats wrote to Ethel Mannin telling her that 'every nerve trembles with horror at what is happening in Europe' and urging her to look up 'The Second Coming' because 'it was written more than sixteen or seventeen years ago and it foretold what is happening'. We sense that Yeats is himself surprised by the prophetic elements of the poem. As Seamus Deane says, the poem 'poses a question in the form of a prophecy; equally it proposes a prophecy in the form of a question'. The prophetic and the interrogatory elements of the poem form a disturbing dialectic that resists the reader's attempt to 'fix' the prophecy in the Book of Revelations or to answer the question with which the poem ends.

Nonetheless, if we remember the three most important factors in literary criticism – 'context, context, context' – the poems surrounding and supporting 'The Second Coming' in the 1921 volume *Michael Robartes and the Dancer* – 'Easter 1916', 'The Leaders of the Crowd', 'Demon and Beast', 'A Prayer for my Daughter', 'A Meditation in Time of War' – tell us how to interpret the best, the worst, the blood dimmed tide and the ceremony of innocence within the Yeatsian system. The poem's very lack of specificity (Bolshevists or Black and Tans?) locates it in the volume but dislocates it from the prophesized contexts of the future where it now finds its relevance.

Does the repetition of 'things fall apart; / the centre cannot hold' in our time make the poem really more applicable to the Iraq War than to Rwanda or Kosovo or Syria? In fact, in 2009, the same headline 'Things fall apart; the centre cannot hold', appeared in *The New York Times* to describe the exodus from the social networking site, Facebook. Just this year in *The Paris Review*, Nick Tabor claimed that '"The Second Coming" may well be the most thoroughly pillaged piece of literature in English', and declared that the hundreds of references to the poem produce a 'feedback loop' that bears little connection to the poem itself. Yeats's modernist anxiety about the centre 'holding' has entered our lingua franca while the first half of the quotation, 'things fall apart' expresses the widespread fear of the endless conflicts of the modern world.

If 'The Second Coming' can be read as the Yeats brand bestseller in ever-proliferating contexts, what happens to poems that are tied to specific historical events and controversies? In considering the phenomenon of the 'quotable Yeats', I discovered that the two most cited poems are 'Easter 1916' and 'The Second Coming'. In other words, the only two lines of Yeats that you will ever need to know are 'A terrible beauty is born' and 'Things fall apart ; / the centre cannot hold'. However, these poems engage with Yeats's theory of heroic history in different ways – 'Easter 1916' is rooted in historical specificity (dates, biographies and names) while 'The Second Coming' specializes in apocalyptic generalities. 'Easter 1916' is usually quoted by Irish journalists or politicians referring either to Irish history after the Rising or to the terror associated with violence in the north and the hope for transformative change. In practice, 'Easter 1916' lends itself to journalistic shorthand about Ireland whereas 'The Second Coming' has universal applicability.

WAS IT FOR THIS?

In 2016, Ireland will celebrate the centenary of the Easter Rising. Writers, journalists, politicians, and citizens will return to the General Post Office (GPO) to remember the moment when Patrick Pearse stood on a chair to read the proclamation of Irish independence. It will be almost impossible to pick up a newspaper without reading Yeats's line 'All changed, changed utterly, / A terrible beauty is born', and once again, the spirit of Cuchulain will stalk through the Post Office. The Ireland that will commemorate the centenary of the Rising has indeed changed utterly. The collapse of the Irish economy in 2008 and the ensuing soaring levels of bank debt, unemployment and emigration have returned Ireland to its pre-Celtic tiger position in the world economy. At the end of 2010, representatives of the International Monetary Fund (IMF) and the

European Central Bank arrived in Dublin to oversee an economic bailout. *The Irish Times* published a leader entitled 'Was it for this?':

> It may seem strange to some that *The Irish Times* would ask whether this is what the men of 1916 died for: a bailout from the German chancellor with a few shillings of sympathy from the British chancellor on the side. There is the shame of it all. Having obtained our political independence from Britain to be the masters of our own affairs, we have now surrendered our sovereignty to the European Commission, the European Central Bank, and the International Monetary Fund.

It was indeed strange to some that the *Irish Times* would ask this question, in this form, in 2010. The piece generated an enormous response including two full pages of letters to the *Irish Times*. Several of these letters referred to the way that the newspaper had reported the Rising itself in Easter week, 1916 as 'an attempt ... to overthrow the constitutional Government of Ireland' and recalled how it had endorsed the triumph of law and order even as the rebel leaders awaited execution in Kilmainham jail.

Of course the *Irish Times* and its readership has not remained static over the last century but nonetheless, the 'Was it for this?' leader is fascinating in its recovery and redeployment of the Easter Rising as the heroic origin of the sovereign nation. For Yeatsians, it was yet more extraordinary that the unacknowledged source for the title of this lament was a familiar line from Yeats's poem 'September 1913', a poem of disappointment in which Yeats accuses contemporary Ireland of betraying its heroic past:

> Was it for this the wild geese spread
> The grey wing upon every tide;
> For this that all that blood was shed,
> For this Edward Fitzgerald died,
> And Robert Emmet and Wolfe Tone,
> All that delirium of the brave?
> Romantic Ireland's dead and gone,
> It's with O'Leary in the grave.

We might well ask what the *Irish Times* is communicating by quoting Yeats's 1913 assessment of Ireland's failures almost a century later and also consider how we evaluate the connection between these two historical moments?

The line under scrutiny here, 'Was it for this?' is a rhetorical question where the important question mark is withheld until Yeats intensifies his outrage by repeating 'for this'. 'This' draws our attention to the present moment of the poem's publication, the prevailing cultural and political conditions that have incurred the poet's wrath. Critics such as Nicholas Grene and George Bornstein have drawn attention to the 'thick political codings' surrounding the original publication of 'September 1913' in the letters column of the *Irish Times* as part of Yeats's protracted intervention on behalf of the Hugh Lane / Municipal Gallery controversy. Entitled 'Romance in Ireland (on reading much of the correspondence against the Art Gallery)', the poem had a polemical purpose – to rebuke those who would deny funds to the project unless it 'were proved the people wanted pictures'. Yeats's enemies are those who would 'pray and save,' the materialist, uncultured Catholic middle classes, and their representative, William Martin Murphy (proprietor of the *Irish Independent* and the *Irish Press*). Yet, when the poem was published in *Responsibilities* as 'September 1913', the effect was to erase the specific context of the Lane pictures and instead to foreground the poem's indictment of its readers for their lack of courage, passion, and heroism. The particularities of the cultural betrayal of the Gallery are transposed to a general betrayal of the ideals of 1798, invoking the heroic Anglo-Irish lineage of Emmet, Fitzgerald, and Tone as well as the Fenian leader, John O'Leary. The poem becomes a 'state of the nation' address anchored by its title to calendrical time but devoted to the mythical timeline of heroic history.

Yeats's hasty consignment of 'Romantic Ireland' to the grave in 1913 was necessarily revised by the events of 1916. His changing perspective on the historical relevance of the poem's chorus is evident in the 'Note' he added in July 1916 to the group of Municipal Gallery poems:

> 'Romantic Ireland's dead and gone' sounds old-fashioned now. It seemed true in 1913, but I did not foresee 1916. The late Dublin Rebellion, whatever one can say of its wisdom, will long be remembered for its heroism. 'They weighed so lightly what they gave', and gave too, in some cases, without hope of success.

In allowing that 'September 1913' sounds 'old-fashioned' in the light of the grand heroic gesture of the 1916 Rising, Yeats invokes the different temporal frameworks of history – historical acts, current events and the sense of posterity claimed by future memory. We can see this too in 'Easter 1916' in which the date as title invites the reader to meditate on the transformative effect of the event on historical time. The poem's ambiguity rests not just in the oxymoron of the refrain but also in its negotiation of the past of the unremarkable rebels, the present of the Rising and the time to be of anticipated remembrance.

The same timelines affect the resurrection of 'September 1913' in the contemporary moment to berate Irish politicians and the electorate for their betrayal of the long-buried heroic history of Romantic Ireland.

Buried too is the specific 'this' of Yeats's 1913 question, which included the Dublin lockout as well as the Lane Gallery controversy. But the demonstrative this is also a sweeping gesture of scorn, perhaps even with the American inflexion that accompanies questions – was it for THIS? Yeats's 'this' is the Ireland born of 'huckster's loins,' the Ireland in which Paudeen fumbling in a 'greasy till' has triumphed. It anticipates his later description of his fellow Free State Senators: 'hot and vague, always disturbed, always hating something or other ... They had ... signed the death-warrant[s] of their dearest friend[s] ... Yet their descendants, if they grow rich enough for the travel and leisure that make a finished man, will constitute our ruling class, and date their origin from the Post Office as American families date theirs from the *Mayflower*.' Yeats's scathing allusion to the Post Office and the *Mayflower* and his disdain for the materialism of middle-class Catholic Ireland in 1913 is projected into the future tense where we find ourselves a century later.

The most important question posed by 'September 1913' is not a whodunnit, or who killed romantic Ireland but rather, as Yeats once asked, what do we hope to make of Ireland? Our lost 'this' is the nation-state, the Republic that has surrendered its sovereignty to the European Central Bank and the IMF. It is the anticipated future proclaimed in the GPO in 1916 that has been betrayed rather than the 'Romantic Ireland' of Yeats's dead heroes. Indeed, the fact that the question, 'Was it for this?' posed in 1913 has been so successfully transposed to the 21st century demonstrates Yeats's particular genius for addressing the future or what he calls 'now and in time to be'.

Yeats's silent presence grants authority to the *Irish Times* leader and connects it to the version of Romantic Ireland that he used to browbeat his own contemporaries in 1913. The reference needs no acknowledgement because certain lines by Yeats are so embedded in Irish culture that they have become a collective resource, helping to articulate difficult things. In an age of distrust of political figures and the actions of the state, our poets have become the standard-bearers of our culture, their words more valuable than political placebos.

Of course, when Yeats asked, 'Was it for this?' in September 1913, the men of 1916 had not yet risen or been executed. The central question of the poem was entirely revised by subsequent events. So today as we anticipate the centenary of the Rising, we must also wonder whether our perspective will be radically altered by future events. We have no way of knowing. But we do know that when the eyes of the nation focus on the historically charged space of the GPO in Easter 2016, the iconic statue of Cuchulain will meet its gaze and ask one more important Yeatsian question, '"What then?" sang Plato's ghost. / "What then?"'

Notes on Contributors

Margaret Atwood is the author of more than forty books of fiction, poetry, and critical essays. Her *MaddAddam* trilogy – the Giller and Booker prize-nominated *Oryx and Crake* (2003), *The Year of the Flood* (2009), and *MaddAddam* (2013) – is currently being adapted for HBO. *The Door* (Virago Press, 2007) is her latest volume of poetry. Her novels include *The Blind Assassin*, winner of the Booker Prize (2000); *Alias Grace*, which won the Giller Prize in Canada and the Premio Mondello in Italy; and *The Robber Bride, Cat's Eye, The Handmaid's Tale,* and *The Penelopiad.*

John Banville's novels include *The Book of Evidence, The Sea*, which won the 2005 Man Booker Prize, *Ancient Light*, and, most recently, *The Blue Guitar.* He also writes crime novels under the pen-name Benjamin Black, including *Christine Falls* and *Even the Dead*. He has been awarded the Kafka Prize, the Austrian State Prize for Literature, and the Prince of Asturias Award. His screen-writing credits include *The Sea* and *Albert Nobbs.*

Kevin Barry is the author of the novels *Beatlebone* and *City of Bohane*, and the story collections *Dark Lies The Island* and *There Are Little Kingdoms* (Stinging Fly Press, 2007). He lives in Co Sligo.

Colette Bryce's fourth collection, *The Whole & Rain-domed Universe* (Picador), was shortlisted for the Forward and Costa poetry awards in 2014. Originally from Derry, she currently lives in Newcastle upon Tyne.

Harry Clifton's *The Holding Centre: Selected Poems* 1974-2004 was published in 2014 by Bloodaxe Books. His Ireland Professorship of Poetry lectures, *Ireland and its Elsewheres*, will be published this autumn by UCD Press.

Mary Costello, originally from Galway, lives in Dublin. Her first book, a collection of short stories entitled *The China Factory* (Stinging Fly Press, 2012), was nominated for the 2012 Guardian First Book Award. Her novel *Academy Street* was shortlisted for a Costa Award and named overall Irish Book of the Year 2014.

Catriona Crowe is Head of Special Projects at the National Archives of Ireland, where she has managed the Census Online project. She was on the jury of *A Poem for Ireland*, and was also a judge for the *Irish Times* Poetry Now Award, both in 2015. She is a member of the Royal Irish Academy.

Gerald Dawe has published nine collections of poetry with The Gallery Press, including, most recently, *Selected Poems* (2012) and *Mickey Finn's Air* (2014). *Of War and War's Alarms: Reflections on Modern Irish Writing* will be published by Cork University Press this year.

Martina Evans, poet and novelist, is the author of ten books of prose and poetry. Her latest collection *Burnfort, Las Vegas* (Anvil Press, 2014) was short-listed for the *Irish Times* Poetry Now Award 2015. *Watch*, a pamphlet, will be published by Rack Press in 2016.

Peter Fallon lives in Loughcrew, Co Meath. For more than forty-five years he has edited and published Gallery Books. An award-winning poet, recent publications of his own work include *The Georgics of Virgil* (Oxford World's Classics) and *Strong, My Love* (2014). He is a member of Aosdána and an Honorary Member of the RHA.

Diarmaid Ferriter, Professor of Modern Irish History at UCD, is one of Ireland's best-known historians. His books include *The Transformation of Ireland 1900-2000* (2004), *Occasions of Sin: Sex and Society in Modern Ireland* (2009) and *A Nation and not a Rabble: The Irish Revolution 1913-23* (2015). He is a regular broadcaster on television and radio and a weekly columnist with the *Irish Times*. In 2010 he presented a three-part history of twentieth-century Ireland, *The Limits of Liberty*, for RTÉ television.

Roy Foster is Carroll Professor of Irish History at the University of Oxford and the author of many books, including the two-volume authorised life of WB Yeats, *WB Yeats: A Life, Volume* I: *The Apprentice Mage 1865–1914* (1997) and *Volume II: The Arch-Poet*, 1915–1939 (2003). His most recent book is *Vivid Faces: The Revolutionary Generation in Ireland*, 1890–1923, published last year. He is a well-known broadcaster, reviewer and cultural critic.

Adrian Frazier, Professor emeritus from NUI Galway, is the author of a forthcoming book about Maud Gonne, Lucien Millevoye, and WB Yeats, entitled *The Adulterous Muse*.

John Glenday's first collection, *The Apple Ghost*, won a Scottish Arts Council Book Award and his second, *Undark*, was a Poetry Book Society Recommendation. His third collection, *Grain* (Picador, 2009), was also a Poetry Book Society Recommendation and was shortlisted for both the Ted Hughes Award and the Griffin International Poetry Prize. His collection *The Golden Mean* is forthcoming in September 2015.

Eamon Grennan taught for many years in the English Department of Vassar College. His most recent collections from The Gallery Press are *Out of Breath* and *But the Body*. For the past seven years he has written and directed short *Plays for Voices* for Curlew Theatre Company in Connemara. His forthcoming collection from The Gallery Press is *There Now.*

Tessa Hadley is the author of two short story collections and five novels, including *Accidents in the Home* (2002), and most recently, *The London Train*, (2011), which was a *New York Times* Notable Book. A regular contributor to *The New Yorker* and *Granta*, she lives in Cardiff and teaches at Bath Spa University.

Hugo Hamilton is best known for *The Speckled People* (Fourth Estate, 2003). Described as an 'instant classic', the memoir was published in twenty languages and went on to win numerous prizes. He is a member of Aosdána, and was awarded the *Bundesverdienstkreuz* (Order of Merit) by the German state for his contribution to literature.

Kerry Hardie has published six collections of poetry with The Gallery Press. Her most recent collection, *The Zebra Stood in the Dark* (Bloodaxe Books, 2015), was shortlisted for the *Irish Times* Poetry Now Award. She has published two novels and is currently working on a third.

Margaret Mills Harper is Glucksman Professor of Contemporary Writing in English at the University of Limerick. She is the author of *The Aristocracy of Art in Joyce and Wolfe*, and *Wisdom of Two: The Spiritual and Literary Collaboration of George and WB Yeats*. She co-edited two of the four volumes of Yeats's *Vision* Papers and both the 1925 and the 1937 versions of *A Vision*.

James Harpur has had five books of poetry and one translation (the poems of Boethius) published by Anvil Press. His latest book, *Angels and Harvesters*, was a Poetry Book Society Recommendation and shortlisted for the *Irish Times* Poetry Now prize. He is poetry editor of the *Temenos Academy Review* and a member of Aosdána. He lives in West Cork.

Geraldine Higgins is Associate Professor of English and Director of Irish Studies at Emory University. Her most recent book, *Heroic Revivals from Carlyle to Yeats* (Palgrave, 2012) examines the flexibility of heroic identity in a range of Revival writers. She was the curator of the acclaimed 2014 exhibition 'Seamus Heaney: The Music of What Happens', and in 2016 she will become director of the Yeats International Summer School in Sligo.

Rita Ann Higgins, from Galway, has published ten collections of poetry; the most recent is *Ireland is Changing Mother* (Bloodaxe Books, 2011). *Hurting God*, a memoir in prose and poetry, was published by Salmon Poetry in 2010. Her next collection – *Tongulish* – is due out in 2016 from Bloodaxe Books. She is a member of Aosdána.

Neil Jordan's prose fiction includes *Night in Tunisia*, *The Past*, *The Dream of a Beast*, *Shade* and *Mistaken*. His film credits as writer-director include *The Company of Wolves*, *Mona Lisa*, *Interview with the Vampire* (screenplay by Anne Rice), *The Butcher Boy* and *The Crying Game*, for which he won an Oscar for Best Screenplay.

Thomas Kinsella was born in Dublin in 1928. He attended University College Dublin, entering the Irish Civil Service before becoming a full-time writer and teacher in the United States. He is the author of over thirty collections of poetry, and has translated extensively from the Irish, most notably the great prose epic *The Táin*. The editor of *The New Oxford Book of Irish Verse*, he is also the author of *The Dual Tradition* (Carcanet, 1995), a critical essay on poetry and politics in Ireland. In 2007 he was awarded the freedom of the City of Dublin.

August Kleinzahler's most recent collection of poetry is *The Hotel Oneira* (Faber and Faber/Farrar, Straus and Giroux). He lives in San Francisco.

Alice Lyons, from Paterson, New Jersey, has lived in Sligo and Roscommon since 1998. Her collection *The Breadbasket of Europe* will be published in 2016 by Veer Books, London. She is currently a Fellow in Poetry at the Radcliffe Institute for Advanced Study at Harvard University.

John McAuliffe's fourth book is *The Way In* (The Gallery Press, 2015). He writes a regular poetry column in the *Irish Times* and teaches poetry at the Centre for New Writing at the University of Manchester, where WB Yeats once read to a paying crowd of 600 people.

Campbell McGrath is the author of ten books of poetry, most recently *In the Kingdom of the Sea Monkeys* (Ecco/HarperCollins, 2012), and the forthcoming *XX: Poems for the Twentieth Century* (Ecco/HarperCollins, 2016). He has received numerous awards for his work, including a MacArthur Fellowship and the Kingsley Tufts Award. He holds the Philip and Patricia Frost Professorship in Creative Writing at Florida International University.

Medbh McGuckian was born and still lives in Belfast. She recently retired from teaching at the Seamus Heaney Centre for Poetry and is working on a new volume of poems entitled *Blaris Moor*. Her previous collection *The High Caul Cap* won a Cholmondeley Award. She spends a lot of time in Ballycastle and the Glens of Antrim, which inspire much of her work.

Frank McGuinness, from Buncrana, Co Donegal, is a playwright and novelist who has also published five volumes of poems with The Gallery Press: *Booterstown, The Sea With No Ships, The Stone Jug, Dulse* and, most recently, *In A Town Of Five Thousand People*. He is Professor of Creative Writing at University College Dublin.

Patrick McGuinness's most recent book is *Other People's Countries: A Journey Into Memory* (Jonathan Cape, 2014).

Heather McHugh was born to Canadian parents on the West Coast of the USA. Between 1977 and 2009 she wrote poems, essays, translations and interpretations. For forty years she read literature closely with interested university students, but since 2011 has withdrawn from professional literary pursuits to focus on Caregifted (**www.caregifted.org**).

Bill Manhire lives in Wellington, New Zealand. His *Selected Poems* (2014) is published by Carcanet Press.

Anne Michaels is a poet and novelist. Her books are published in over forty countries and have won many international awards, including the Orange Prize, the Guardian Fiction Prize, and the Lannan Award for Fiction. Her latest book of poetry, *Correspondences* (McClelland and Stewart), was shortlisted for the Griffin Poetry Prize in 2014.

John Montague was born in the United States and brought up in Northern Ireland. He is a poet of international as well as Irish dimensions. His epic *The Rough Field* (1972) is the seminal poem on the Irish Troubles, and he is also an acclaimed love poet. He was appointed the first Ireland Professor of Poetry in 1998, and holds Honorary Doctorates from five universities, including the Sorbonne. Recently he was made a *Chevalier de la Légion d'Honneur*. His *New Collected Poems* appeared in 2012 from The Gallery Press.

Blake Morrison is a poet, novelist, librettist and the author of two bestselling memoirs, *And When Did You Last See Your Father?* and *Things My Mother Never Told Me*. He edited the landmark anthology *The Penguin Book of Contemporary British Poetry* with Andrew Motion. His poetry collections include *Dark Glasses, The Ballad of the Yorkshire Ripper, A Discoverie of Witches,* and *Shingle Street,* published earlier this year. He is Professor of Creative and Life Writing at Goldsmiths College, University of London.

Sinéad Morrissey is the author of five poetry collections. Her most recent collection, *Parallax* (2013), was awarded both the *Irish Times* Poetry Now Prize and the TS Eliot Prize. She lectures in creative writing at the Seamus Heaney Centre for Poetry at Queen's University, Belfast.

Paul Muldoon is the author of twelve books of poetry, most recently *One Thousand Things Worth Knowing* (Faber and Faber, 2015). He has received both the Pulitzer Prize for Poetry and the TS Eliot Prize.

Richard Murphy was born in his grandfather's house near Kilmaine, Co Mayo, eighty-eight years ago. For the past seven years he has lived at a friend's house on the edge of a paddy field in the highlands of Sri Lanka, where he welcomes visitors. In 2013 Lilliput Press and Bloodaxe Books jointly published his *Poems 1952–2012*.

Eiléan Ní Chuilleanáin is an Emeritus Fellow of Trinity College, Dublin, where she has taught since 1966. Her collection *The Sun-Fish* was shortlisted for the TS Eliot Prize and won the Griffin International Prize for Poetry in 2010; *The Boys of Bluehill* was published this year by The Gallery Press. She is a founder and co-editor of the Irish poetry journal *Cyphers*.

Joseph O'Connor is a novelist and Professor of Creative Writing at the University of Limerick. WB Yeats appears as a character in his novel *Ghost Light* (2010).

Bernard O'Donoghue is a former Director of the Yeats International Summer School in Sligo. His most recent book of poems is *Farmers Cross* (Faber and Faber, 2011).

Sharon Olds, a Californian poet, has published twelve collections of poetry, including *Satan Says* (1980), *The Dead and The Living* (1984), *The Wellspring* (1996), and *Stag's Leap* (2012), which won both the Pulitzer and TS Eliot Prizes. Olds was New York State Poet Laureate from 1998 to 2000, and is currently a Professor at New York University.

Olivia O'Leary is a broadcaster and journalist. She presents a political column for RTÉ Radio 1's *Drivetime* programme. Two collections of columns, *Party Animals* and *Politicians and Other Animals,* have been published by The O'Brien Press.

Joseph O'Neill's latest novel is *The Dog* (Pantheon / Fourth Estate, 2014).

Fintan O'Toole is literary editor of the *Irish Times*. His most recent book is *A History of Ireland in 100 Objects* (2013).

Molly Peacock is included in *The Oxford Book of American Poetry*, and is the author of six volumes of poetry, including *The Second Blush* and *Cornucopia: New and Selected Poems,* both published by WW Norton and Co (USA and UK), and McClelland and Stewart (Canada). Her latest book of nonfiction is *The Paper Garden: An Artist Begins Her Life's Work at 72* (McClelland and Stewart / Bloomsbury). Her most recent book of stories is *Alphabetique: 26 Characteristic Fictions* (McClelland and Stewart).

Sheenagh Pugh is half Welsh, half Irish but now lives in Shetland. She has published many collections with Seren; her latest was *Short Days, Long Shadows* (Seren 2014).

Nell Regan's debut collection *Preparing for Spring* (Arlen House) was shortlisted for the Glen Dimplex New Writing, Strong/Shine, Patrick Kavanagh, and Vincent Buckley Awards. Her latest collection is *One Still Thing* (Enitharmon Press). She has been a Fellow at the International Writing Programme, Iowa, and a recipient of a Fulbright Scholar Award.

Denise Riley's poetry features in *Penguin Modern Poets* 10 (1996) along with Douglas Oliver and Iain Sinclair. *Denise Riley: Selected Poems* was published by Reality Street in 2000. Her non-fiction publications include *War in the Nursery: Theories of the Child and Mother* (1983); *'Am I that Name?' Feminism and the Category of 'Women' in History* (1988); and *Time Lived, Without Its Flow* (2012).

Maurice Riordan's collections include *The Water Stealer* (2013) and *The Holy Land* (2007), from Faber and Faber. He has also edited *The Finest Music: Early Irish Lyrics* (Faber and Faber, 2014). Born in Lisgoold, Co Cork, he lives in London and is editor of *The Poetry Review*.

Chris Russell lives in New York City and works in the field of deaf-blindness and special education. He illustrates contributors' portraits for *Stonecutter: A Journal of Art and Literature*, and is currently working on a graphic translation of Witold Gombrowicz's *Cosmos*, forthcoming from Siglio Press.

Donal Ryan holds the 2015 Arts Council Writer-in-Residence Fellowship at the University of Limerick. His debut novel *The Spinning Heart* won the *Guardian* First Book Award (2013), was long-listed for the 2013 Man Booker Prize and the Desmond Elliott Prize, and was a finalist for the 2014 IMPAC Dublin Literary Award. His second novel, *The Thing About December*, was also a number one bestseller. His first short story collection, *A Slanting of the Sun*, will be published worldwide in September 2015.

Philip Schultz's most recent book is a novel in verse, *The Wherewithal*. His poetry collection, *Failure*, won the Pulitzer prize in 2008. His poem in this issue, 'The Books of Dead Friends', will appear in a forthcoming collection, *Luxury*. He is the founder and director of a private writing school, The Writers Studio, based in New York City and online.

Vijay Seshadri is the author of four collections of poems: *Wild Kingdom, The Long Meadow,* and *3 Sections* (Graywolf Press), and *The Disappearances: New and Selected Poems* (HarperCollins India); and numerous essays, reviews, and memoir fragments. His work has been recognized with a number of honours, including the Pulitzer Prize for Poetry in 2014.

Gerard Smyth's collections of poetry include *A Song of Elsewhere* (Dedalus Press, 2015), and *The Fullness of Time: New and Selected Poems* (Dedalus Press, 2010). He was the 2012 recipient of the O'Shaughnessy Poetry Award and is co-editor (with Pat Boran) of *If Ever You Go: A Map of Dublin in Poetry and Song* (Dedalus Press), Dublin's One City One Book in 2013. He is a member of Aosdána and Poetry Editor of the *Irish Times*.

Adam Thorpe is a poet, novelist, essayist and translator. His most recent volume of poetry is *Voluntary* (Jonathan Cape, 2012). His novels include *Ulverton* (1992, reissued recently as a Vintage Classic), and *Flight* (Jonathan Cape, 2012). His first work of non-fiction, *On Silbury Hill,* was published to great acclaim by Little Toller Books last year.

Colm Tóibín is Irene and Sidney B Silverman Professor of the Humanities at Columbia University. He is the author of eight novels and two collections of stories. His most recent book, *On Elizabeth Bishop,* is published by Princeton University Press.

Jeffrey Wainwright's most recent book of poems is *The Reasoner* (Carcanet, 2012) and a new book is due in 2016. He is also the author of *Poetry: The Basics* (Third edition, Routledge, 2015), and of a book of essays on the poetry of Geoffrey Hill, *Acceptable Words* (Manchester University Press, 2005). He lives in Manchester.

Rosanna Warren teaches in the Committee on Social Thought at the University of Chicago. Her most recent book of poems is *Ghost in a Red Hat* (WW Norton and Co, 2011).

Bill Whelan has composed music across many genres including orchestral, Irish traditional, jazz, and choral, and he has written for film and theatre. He wrote the original music for Yeats's plays for the WB Yeats International Theatre Festival in 1989, and subsequently set to music poems by Michael Coady, Nuala Ní Dhomhnaill, Paul Durcan, Peter Fallon, Michael Hartnett, Michael Longley, Derek Mahon, and Frank McGuinness. He taught a course on setting words to music with Paul Muldoon at Princeton University.

Rowan Williams was born in South Wales and has studied and taught in Cambridge and Oxford. After ten years as Archbishop of Canterbury, he became Master of Magdalene College, Cambridge, in 2013. His most recent collection of poetry is *The Other Mountain* (Carcanet, 2014).

Maud Gonne Crossword (p. 176)

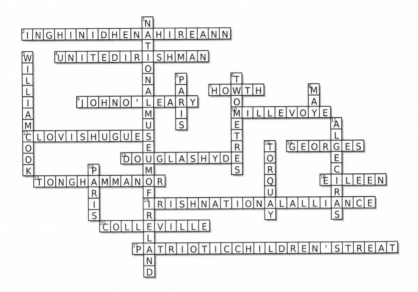

How Yeats Are You? (p. 59)

0-20   WB Yikes! You need emergency Yeatsifying. Start with *A Vision*, (the easy stuff), and take it from there.

21-30   WB Yeast! It's getting hot in here. Your score's spinning like a perne in a gyre. (Though, like Maud Gonne, you still leave something to be desired).

31-40   WB Yes! You're more Yeats than Yeats himself – he scored exactly zero, via ouija board.

Yeats Quiz (p. 108)

1 c.   2 c.   3 b.   4 d.   5 b.   6 c.   7 c   Joined a in 1889, b in 1890, d in 1911. 8 c.   9 d.   10 a.   11 c.   12 d.   13 a: WWI; b: the Easter Rising; c: the Irish Civil War; d: WWII.   14 c.   15 d.   16 b.